SOUTH LONDON

Edited by Steve Twelvetree

First published in Great Britain in 2003 by
YOUNG WRITERS
Remus House,
Coltsfoot Drive,
Peterborough, PE2 9JX
Telephone (01733) 890066

HB ISBN 0 75434 217 4
SB ISBN 0 75434 218 2

FOREWORD

This year, the Young Writers' The Write Stuff! competition proudly presents a showcase of the best poetic talent from over 40,000 up-and-coming writers nationwide.

Young Writers was established in 1991 and we are still successful, even in today's modern world, in promoting and encouraging the reading and writing of poetry.

The thought, effort, imagination and hard work put into each poem impressed us all, and once again, the task of selecting poems was a difficult one, but nevertheless, an enjoyable experience.

We hope you are as pleased as we are with the final selection and that you and your family continue to be entertained with *The Write Stuff! South London* for many years to come.

CONTENTS

Alleyn's School

Jonathan Berry	58
Brian Wong	59
Angeli Jeyarajah	60
Natalie Fiennes	60
Hamish Hunter	61
Yudhisthra Singh	62
Lucie O'Mara	62
Kit Hawkins	63
William Chapman	63
Oliver Furber	64
Vida Scannell	65
Lottie Unwin	66
Maksim Mijovic	66
Max Hart-Walsh	67
Hannah Waldegrave	68
Freddie Smith	68
Chloë Courtney	69
Hannah Ewens	70
Hugo Jackson	71
Ben Chapman	72
Melissa Chan	72
Christina Lees	73
George Trickey	74
Charlotte Anderson	75
Saffron Clague	76
Miranda Willis	76
William Bedingfield	77

Bredinghurst School

Damola George	77
Dominick George	77
Mayo Makinde	78
Segun Bolodeoku	78
Ryan O'Sullivan	79
Kris Porter	79
Leigh Smith	80

Charlton School (SEN)

Joe Bhatia	80
Michael Uwah	80
Darren Lynch	81
Kayleigh Bennison	81
Sam Beard	82
Maria Whitefield	83
Tommy Rogers	83

Chestnut Grove School

Rhianna Crawford	83
Daniel West	84
Darrel Doyle	84
Oscar Brazil	85
Abigail Wighton	86
Stuart Watkinson	86
Verneece Hilaire	87
Santhokie Nagulendran	88
Zainab Kauroo	89
Amy Mutch	89
Daniel Gurney	90
Johanne Williams	90
Gemma Tester	91
Stantelle Collins	92
Charelle Christian	93
Zirena Walker	94
Alissa Abena	95
Katherine Drake	95
Ruth N'Choh	96
James Armian	97
Samina Bhatti	98
Elicia Gayle Bouncer	99
Sezin Taner	100
Andrew Webber	100
Ana Almeida	101
Jade Llewellyn	101
Ieva Adomaviciute	102
Ismel Boateng	102

The Poems

WWW.MYPOEM.COM

Why won't the computer start?
I thought turning the power off was smart,
Now where's that Microsoft Office icon?
Every time I need it, it's gone,
Maybe it's inside the what do you call it. com.

Over your limit on the C drive collection,
Delete some files to revive your connection.

Press start to finish,
Pop down menus,
Yahoo and Google are on the screen,
The mouse is stuck inside my dream,
Pent up in my Pentium.

What do you mean my connection has failed?
Does that mean it wasn't mailed?

@ this time of day,
On my computer I play,
Backslash, forwardslash,
You've got mail,
Isn't that such a nice detail!

Hypertext links, embedded text.
Goodness what'll they think of next!

ISDN to see you soon,
HTML I have to go,
JAVA nice day!
DVD now,
I must ROM!

Jennifer Gleeson (12)
Alleyn's School

GROOVY GRANNY

When I am old and wrinkly,
I will don moon boots
And perhaps a Stetson,
And a Mickey Mouse hat which says 'Boo' if you pull the ears.
I'll spend my pension on yo-yos and snakeskin boots
And gold patent sandals and yodel,
'We ain't got no money for bills!'
And when I
Temporarily
Run out of energy
I'll plonk myself in the middle of the pavement
And when I'm fully charged again,
I'll wolf down egg salad sarnies and prod
Fat men in their tummies.
When it's absolutely freezing cold, I'll
Run down the street
In my leopardskin bikini
And pick the food in bearded men's beards,
And learn to ride a motorbike like a Hell's Angel
And drink tea like posh ladies.

I can wear foul clothes and grow facial hair
And eat three ounces of raw meat in one go,
Or only eat chocolate and crisps for a day,
And collect leather jackets and dentures and knee socks
And chocolate creams.

But now we have clothes that keep us from going senile . . .
And pay our mortgages and remember to say,
'Yes Sir, thank you, Sir,'
And set a good example by not listening to bad 80s music.
We must wear furry catsuits to dinner and read and reread
David Beckham's biography until we can quote from it.

But maybe I should groove a bit now?
So my cronies aren't too upset that their fluorescent shellsuits
are not 'in' anymore,
When suddenly I am old and wrinkly and don moon boots
And perhaps a Stetson.

Lily Thomas (12)
Alleyn's School

BORIS

(Dedicated to my cat, Boris)

The black shadow moves through the night,
Lurking in the dark.

The black shadow spies a mouse running down the road,
He follows it quietly, prepares to pounce, always alert.

The black shadow returns home, trophy in his mouth,
Leaves it at the bottom of the stairs.

The black shadow was my cat, Boris, bringing me a present,
Boris was very gentle, an elegant and handsome cat.

The black shadow used to sit in my bed in the morning,
This all stopped about three weeks ago.

The black shadow was out in the street again, lurking in the dark,
He saw his mother across the road and ran out to go and see her.

The black shadow did not see the Jeep roaring down the road,
How could it have dodged it?

The black shadow lay in the road, broken,
That was my cat, Boris, but now he is no more . . .

Luke Warren (13)
Alleyn's School

MY THOUGHTS

In this day and age,
You hear all sorts of horrible things,
On the news,
On radios,
Things happening,
To people,
To children,
Wars in countries.
All we do,
Is wait
And hope,
That it will all suddenly
Disappear.
Why don't we do anything to help?
Because we,
Don't *want* to know.
In Third World countries,
Children are starving,
Even dying,
While we throw away,
What we don't *want*.
You sometimes hear,
On TV,
Such monstrosities,
As child prostitution.
It's almost unbearable,
To think,
What some little children,
Sometimes as young,
As seven or eight,
Go through,
Every day of their lives,
When all they really want,
Is to go home
To their parents.

But they are unable to,
They live too far away,
They can't afford it.
At the end of the day,
They don't have any one,
To give them a hug,
Ask about their day.
No parent to tell them,
They're wonderful,
Or beautiful,
Or special.
Our society today,
Is so demanding,
You must have a perfect body,
Face,
Otherwise,
You get nowhere.
But if we've all just stopped,
And thought,
For a while,
About things,
Like do I need that,
Or do I want that?
Just make sure,
That when you leave the world,
It's a better place,
Than when you came into it.

Kitty McGilchrist (12)
Alleyn's School

THE DOGS STRIKE BACK

The wolf whistled,
the wind howled,
the boy barked,
and dog bowed.
Not a feline creature to be seen,
not a king, not a queen,
astonishment filled the air,
fear was smelt everywhere.
Boys fetched bones and girls did tricks,
dogs would walk humans,
humans would catch sticks,
but in a shed,
some humans were,
as they had fled,
escaped the fur.
They would fight for human rights,
they'd tell each human what to do,
by running there,
fro and to.
The humans agreed to do their best,
they'd make it known,
for kind men and pests,
to fight the dogs and put things right,
This only happened just last night
when the wind whistled.
The wolf howled,
the dog barked,
and the boy bowed.
A feline creature was to be seen,
sleeping in a feathered dream.

Keziah Lewis (11)
Alleyn's School

THE DAWN OF DARKNESS

What causes pollution, poverty and starvation?
It is one thing.
Ever since the dawn of industry,
The planet's doom has been carved in stone.
Will our great, great grandchildren ever live to see
the lush green forests, that are now so few?
Or will they just be a memory, caught in a photo?
Surely now it is clear what the fate of the Earth is,
But our chance is nearly gone,
Gone in a flash of greed and carelessness.

What causes extinction, sadness and wars?
It is one thing.
The power to stop this has been passed down
through the hands of everyone,
But it has been dropped.
Why? Because of greed and ignorance.
Everyone has a value, anyone can change the future.

What causes the end?
It is one thing.
The ice will melt, all through not considering the future.
Now what barriers will hold the floods back?
It was not the inventor, it was the user.
It was not who began it, it was who ended it.
Who will be alive in the next million years to tell the fairy stories
of the beautiful forests and the cold snow?
For that is all it will be.
The most valuable possession squandered,
But remember,
When you think it's happening,
It's already happened!

Alexandra Hamilton (11)
Alleyn's School

THE GOBLIN

A slimy creature comes out at night,
I bet you have never seen such a sight,
Its feet are the darkest of pitch-black
It goes to sleep in an old mouldy sack.

The goblin isn't like the creatures in fairy tales,
Just for a light snack it has worms and snails.
It will tear you apart, limb from limb,
Watch out! You may be its next victim.

Its eyes are a shade of dazzling gold,
Its ears are pointy, they stand out bold.
Never underestimate the power of its jaws,
Or the sharpness of its gnarly claws.

The goblin isn't like the creatures in fairy tales,
Just for a light snack it has worms and snails,
It will tear you apart, limb from limb,
Watch out! You might be its next victim.

Sam Eade (12)
Alleyn's School

FOXES

They come, they go
Crouching so low,
They play, they fight
All through the night.

But in the day they are more wary
People and cars they find quite scary,
They eat whatever food they find
Hunger is always on their mind.

They find survival very tough
Although at times life's not so rough,
New cubs are born, they play, they run
I love to sit and watch their fun.

Maria-Gioia Gowar (12)
Alleyn's School

BEND IT LIKE BECCA

Football is a funny game,
I've played it all my life,
I don't know how it happened,
It started with my wife.
She said one day, 'Why don't
You play, a game to get you slim?
Go out and kick a ball or at least
Go to the gym.'
The gym, it seemed like hard work,
I didn't fancy it at all,
But then one day whilst
Clearing out, I came across a
Ball, 'Yippee!' I yelled and put
On my shorts and ran to
My friend, Ray,
'Please, please,' I said, 'in your
New team, the football, can
I play?'
And that's how it started,
With me in the team,
My love for football began to gleam
And now to everyone,
I say, 'I'll play football
Until my dying day.'

Rebecca Cope (12)
Alleyn's School

MISTAKEN IDENTITY

'Do you think you can sing?'
The advert said, and I did
but not very well.
I went to the audition
Then I heard 'Next!' and 'Good Luck!'
I thought if I smiled
and looked cool, I might score,
especially with my pink and green hair.
But my smile wore thin
when they asked for my flute.
Then I creased as I clocked;
I'd arrived at the wrong stage door!
I had wanted to shine as a pop star goddess,
not a wind instrument - third from the left!
They said, 'There's the floor.'
So I said, 'Where's the door?'
But was through it before they replied.

Hannah Lederer Alton (12)
Alleyn's Senior School

TO BOOK, WITH ALL MY LOVE XXX

Book is always there,
Book is always there,
Book is ready to open up
And show me what's inside.

Book is thin and short,
But book is kind and gentle.
Book's skin is a pale brown,
Book is soft and tranquil.

I love Book, Book will tell me;
All about myself.
Book will always be there,
Book will always be there.

Sarah Burke (12)
Alleyn's School

PEOPLE

Wars bring death,
Seas people need,
Yet people pollute seas
And have wars,
Why?

Some people kill other people,
Some people kill animals,
Some people are dangerous,
Why?

Some people keep animals locked up,
Some people pollute,
Some people cut down trees,
Some people are stupid,
Why?

Some people judge people
For what they look like.
Some people are racist,
Why?

Some people are kind . . .
To nature -
They don't exist,
Why?

Luke Staden (11)
Alleyn's School

THE WATERFALL

Pouncing, pounding here and there,
Thundering mostly everywhere,
Closer and closer the fall comes,
The bursting water loudly hums.

Down, down,
Water descends,
Plunging down,
It never ends,
Tension rises,
In gigantic sizes,
Until she . . .

Booms, clashes, loudly smashes,
She brakes harshly with a lot of noise,
She's getting silent, tranquil and still,
The water has now had its fill.

Srijan Thakur (11)
Alleyn's School

THE LITTLE OLD SWING

There it swayed in the wind,
Shivering when it snowed,
Baking when it was hot.
Everyone went to it for fun,
Even the adults who made its rope strain.

But one day it fell,
Decades falling, fallen.
It had been there for ever,
The little old swing.

Hannah Houston (12)
Alleyn's School

PEOPLE TEASE AND LAUGH AT ME

People tease and laugh at me
They say I cannot spell
I know I have dyslexia
Which makes my life sheer hell.

People tease and laugh at me
They take my money and demand more
But I have none to give them
As my family are very poor.

People tease and laugh at me
Saying my clothes are second-hand
But they are only jealous
Why? I do not understand.

People tease and laugh at me
They beat me up and make me cry
Now I'm in hospital
Feeling like I want to die.

Adam Collins (11)
Alleyn's School

FUN

Swimming is fun and I know it,
Reading is fun and I know it,
Cycling is fun and I know it,
School is fun and I know it,
But,
Homework is boring and I know it!

Leela Paul (12)
Alleyn's School

A HOLE

I heard it clear, I heard the tear,
Inside me, I know there's a hole somewhere.
I felt the rain come tumbling through
And I counted the droplets: one-hundred and two.

I heard it clear, heard the tear,
Inside me, I know there's a hole somewhere.
I felt the wind come blowing through me at a gale,
It was like a fantasy, a fairy tale.

I heard it clear, I heard the tear,
Inside me, I know there's a hole somewhere.
The crisp snow fell and turned to ice,
This feeling wasn't at all nice.

I heard it clear, I heard the tear,
Inside me, I know there's a hole somewhere.
The leaves turned to brown and fell from the tree,
Oh, why did this ever have to happen to me?

I heard it clear, I heard the tear,
Inside me, I know there's a hole somewhere.
The bright little daffodils were blooming by plenty,
I suddenly realised, that it was my heart that was empty.

I heard it loud, I heard the sound,
The thing I needed, I had found.
I felt the love come streaming fast,
What I wanted had come at last.

Annie Clarke (11)
Alleyn's School

MY FANTASY

The world is an amazing place, so many things to see,
Everything that's living there, including you and me.
Raindrops glistening on grass like crystals,
Clouds floating in the sky in handfuls and fistfuls.
Hands held, that will never part,
Happiness and smiles from the bottom of your heart.
Children laugh and run about,
Wisdom that is passed from mouth to mouth.
People look into the sky,
And happiness shall pass through their eyes.
Babies are born and the older die,
People laugh with happiness and with sadness, cry.
People shake hands and peace is made,
One smiles to another, their friendship won't fade.
No eyes to mop, no mouths to feed,
Everyone's equal, no one is in need.
Skin black or white, it's just the same,
Nobody's different, just like each drop of rain.
Making peace, no war to fight,
No darkness in our hearts, all is light.
The grass, a crisp green, the sky, a rough blue,
The world is a rainbow, around me and you.
The sun is a diamond in the sky,
All is truth, no one speaks a lie.
The fish in the sea, the animals on the ground,
Everyone respects the living things around.
Somebody looks round and admires the Earth,
Because they understand what life is worth.

Holly Naden (11)
Alleyn's School

THE DRUMMER

My brother is a drummer,
he drums all day and night.
He practises in my room,
he thinks he has a right.
If you try and stop him,
he puts up a good fight.

My brother pounds with passion
he gives it all his soul.
He plays in every fashion
to jazz and rock and roll.
I wish he'd play the trumpet,
or the guitar instead.
My brother has no drum set,
he drums right on my head.

Felix Turnbull-Walter (11)
Alleyn's School

FIELDS OF SPRING

Lying on a bed of roses,
Sitting in a field of posies
Once bare branches,
Now blossomed with leaves
The sun shines warmly,
With a chilly, frosty breeze
Animals emerge from their holes,
Rabbits, mice, badgers and moles
The grass sprouts, lush and green
The field of spring is a beautiful scene.

Meriel Hodgson-Teall
Alleyn's School

SNOW FALL

In the black
of the night, tons of white specks fall
from the sky.
Everyone of them different
from the other.
They tumble down, slowly
twisting and turning
as they fall
like tiny flying ballerinas.
They cover the land
in a blanket of white.
The ground sparkles under the moon,
all is silent,
until,
the sun advances over the horizon
the freshly fallen snow dazzling
in the light.
The sunlight pours through windows
and wakes sleeping children
they go to the window
and gasp
at the beauty.

Thomas Albrow-Owen (11)
Alleyn's School

THE WIND

Howling wind buffeting, buffeting
stirring leaves, lashing sea tide
howling wind, shrieking, shrieking
blowing along, birds fly alongside.

Bea Domenge (11)
Alleyn's School

THE OCEAN

The ocean roars at me,
The ocean roars at me.

When the ocean is calm
He is protective,
But if the ocean is angry,
He is destructive.

Ocean can be vicious.
He dribbles like never before.
His gigantic claw swallows me whole,
As his enormous mouth opens wide.

Also Ocean can become very warm,
He gives you a comforting look.
He tries to wave at me,
As he smiles at me in the evening sun.

The ocean roars at me,
The ocean roars at me.

Michael Zhuang (12)
Alleyn's School

DID YOU EVER WONDER?

Did you ever wonder,
Or think that it was odd,
That the sound of thunder
Might have come from God?

Did you ever wonder,
Or did you ever know,
That if you cooled down water,
It could turn out as snow?

Did you ever wonder,
Or think that it was fun,
To lie around in the heat
And soak up all the sun?

I have always wondered,
I don't know about you,
But where does weather come from?
Do you think you know too?

Emma Dawe (12)
Alleyn's School

MY RIDDLE

Beneath my hard but fragile coating, lies my secret,
How things would be so different,
If only my mother had time to care, to love me
I would wear a different coat,
I could see the world
And my voice would be heard.

Because of all this, I can be treated badly,
Beaten up, bashed about with steel, scalded.
Still, I do not scream or show my pain.

Why, after all this, do I still manage to have
A bright, sunny, coloured centre to my personality?
Is it because I am a fool,
Or is it because I have no choice?

What am I?

Answer: An egg.

Michael Maullin (12)
Alleyn's School

SORRY DAD

I'm sorry Dad, please don't get annoyed
This has been driving me mad!
I'm sorry Dad, please don't get upset now,
I've done something really bad!

I don't know what to say,
I've been racking my brains all day!
I don't know how to tell you in a better way!

I'll tell you straight, straight what I've done,
But believe me Dad, it was just for fun!

I'm sorry Dad, please don't get annoyed,
This is really hard!
I'm sorry, Dad, please don't get upset now
I stole your credit card!

I was buying pretty dresses!
I was buying high-heeled shoes!
I was buying so much stuff that it was really hard to choose!

Mabel Holland (11)
Alleyn's School

THE SUN

The sun is big, round and powerful,
Helping us when we work and play.
She crowns us all with warmth and happiness
And stays with us through the day.

Never giving up,
A glowing coin, she shines strong.
We feel her presence when we are alone,
From country to country she speeds along.

She overpowers the wind and rain,
Never feeling isolated.
She knows her job,
To keep the world forever . . .

Lauren Rosamond (13)
Alleyn's School

WHY?

Why do all the people cry and why
do they all die?
Why has everyone's sense of
laughter gone and been replaced
with depression?
Why is it that when I read the
newspaper, Posh and Becks are
more important than children
dying in Third World countries?
Why does the world go through so
much suffering and yet we soon forget?
Why do children scream as their
parents abuse them and so we
turn a blind eye?
Why let the world go through so
much pain and because it doesn't
affect you, you have no reason to help?
Why hurt other people with
your spitefulness?
Why torture others so you can
have your way at every
possible chance?

Jameela Raymond (12)
Alleyn's School

THE SHADOW

The shadow sulks around,
Coated in darkness and evil.
It wears nothing but black,
And stalks its target.

It takes pleasure from its sport,
And it will terrify you.
You will feel watched every hour of the day,
And become too frightened to leave your house.

Then it pounces,
And pulls you deep into the fiery caverns of Hell.
There it tortures you,
In every way possible.

It is a stalker,
You cannot escape it.
It will get you,
And when it does you will never see the light of day again.

Victoria Bentley (11)
Alleyn's School

THE WORLD'S HARDEST EVER TEST!

I opened the black school doors
And was pleased to have met Ms Crew
The cleverest person I knew.

'Oh please help me!
I'm in such a bother
I did not study, not even for my mother.

Please can I copy
And sit next to you
So I get good marks and sleep like you too?'

'No of course not, it's out of the question.'
'Fine then,' I replied as I'd been bitten by a fox
'I'll just have to say I have chickenpox!'

Stuart Blair (12)
Alleyn's School

I HATE MY PARENTS

I hate my parents
They always yell at me
It's, 'Do this,' 'Do that,'
'Make me a cup of tea!'

I hate my parents
They make me do my homework
And if it isn't done
They shout and go berserk

They make me practise the piano
They make me eat my greens
And if I don't, I get in trouble
They're always really mean

I suppose they buy my food
And have bought me everything I have
And they give me chocolate
I guess they're not *that* bad!

Polly Doodson (12)
Alleyn's School

BALLET

'Toes pointed, ribs relaxed,
The energy in your body lacks!
Tummies in, knees stretched,
Your smile is never too far-fetched.
Your pirouettes need some work;
You look as if you're going to lurch,
Your back is hunched and tighten up less,
For if you don't you're in a mess!
Take that scrunchie out of your hair, it's nice all plain,
I don't care if you think I'm insane.
Pliés girls, get out the barre,
In the middle, not too far.
Bend, stretch, rise and down,
Lighten up and *please* don't frown.
Battement Tondue, *stretch those feet*,
First position's supposed to meet.
Grande Battement throw, and soft, throw and soft,
Come on, concentrate, and please don't cough!
Look girls, please don't gasp,
After class water bottles you can clasp.
We are nearly finished, now chassé coupe chassé hop,
One by one, don't delay -
You know we haven't got all day!
Goodbye and au revoir,
And I'll see you next week at the barre!'

Francesca Gray-Walkinshaw (12)
Alleyn's School

SEASONS

W inter is the time for smoky fires,
I lie upon the woollen rug,
N obody around the Christmas tree,
T oday, we are wrapped up, all nice and snug
E verybody plays in the snow
R acing hearts, no one in bed with a Christmas bug!

S pring is a blossoming time,
P eople as well as plants,
R oses red, violets blue
I sing my rhymes, my chants,
N oses red from hayfever,
G o with the flowers and dance.

S ummer, associated with the sun
U ndercover, we are never,
M ums with their babies in the park
M y dog, rarely playing clever,
E veryone, in a cheerful mood,
R ain we won't see ever.

A utumn, the leaves fall,
U nder the trees, lay millions of leaves,
T rees are naked, the cold is near,
U ndiscovered, seen as the man with a rake heaves,
M ammals creep into hibernation,
N o skipping, no falling, no blood from grazed knees.

Georgia Ventiroso (12)
Alleyn's School

IT FEELS LIKE ...

It feels like . . .

Bubbly champagne, fizzing and whizzing
and making me fizz up and pop.

Floating like a balloon into the
endless sky and falling like a raindrop.

Sitting on a silver cloud and
looking down at the world below.

A carefree stream, dripping and trickling
and just being able to flow.

Beautiful snowflakes, with special designs
all silvery-white.

How an eagle must feel, as it soars
through the sky, elegant in flight.

A big white moon, a golden sun
or a sparkling star.

Knowing and understanding
exactly how things are.

I know what it feels like.

I was the first.

Zoë Gelber (12)
Alleyn's School

KITTENS

Kittens like to play,
They'll play all day,
They get stuck up trees,
They try to catch bees.

They sit on your face,
They hide in every place,
They scratch your best friend,
They just drive you round the bend!

They scatter their hair,
Absolutely everywhere,
Most of all they sleep,
Sleep without a peep.

When you stroke their hair into a spike,
They purr like a motorbike!
When you feed them food,
They come in speedy,
They push each other out being very greedy.

The rest of the time they stay out late,
You leave them to their own fate,
Until in the morning,
When they climb on your bed,
Then ouch!
They've jumped on your head!

Harry Savell (12)
Alleyn's School

THE HOUNDS OF THE HOWL

Eyes aglow in the silver moonlight,
Amber, alert and intelligent,
Carefully listening.
Fangs as keen as a knife's edge,
Fur all sleek, black, grey and white,
Silently stalking.
Here are the lords of the night.

An elite force of army commandos,
Preparing their surprise attack,
Weapons awaiting.
Tracking their prey for long hours,
Soon is the time - no holding back,
Straining their senses.
Silence in the forest, so black.

Pointed needles on the end of light footpaws
And a snarl that warns others of ill,
Danger looming.
Target becomes aware, signal is given,
The brothers break the protective circle,
Eager and expectant
And the leader charges forward to kill.

A triumphant howl in the dark of night
And relief, for hunger will be held at bay,
Appetites astounding.
And so the pack feasts until morning light,
Nurturing their young, families united,
Satisfaction surrounding.
They are the lords of the night.

Jack Kelleher (11)
Alleyn's School

LOVE ME, LOVE ME NOT!

Sometimes I wish I was loud,
I wish I could chase away the rain and clouds.

Love can't give up this time,
To the depths of the Earth you're mine.

Things are trying to settle down,
Just trying to figure exactly what I'm all about.

But you'll never see inside,
Until you realise what I am.

Fall back and take a look at me,
If you do you could only see!
I'm real, I'll feel what only I can feel!

Please believe me, take me seriously!
But I fear you're only telling me things that I want to hear.

Staring back at my life those days when I cried,
And into the vibe I'm walking through I know I've tried.

I'm staring at my face, my cheeks have gone all red,
I'm searching for the words inside my head.

I don't need your doubt in me,
So if you're going, please let me be!

I wish I could make cures for how people are,
I finished abruptly even though I got so far.

If you could only see,
I want to change the world for you and me.

I wish I could get pain away if I cry,
I wish I was you not I!

Grace Fletcher (11)
Alleyn's School

FAME

Everyone dreams
Fame is the word,
Fame is the fashion
Which lives forever.

You and me,
Kylie and Britney
Lives so different
But very alike.

They are hunted
By the press
You and me
By brothers and sisters.

Hiding away from the hounds,
Don't say the wrong word,
Don't make the wrong move.
Or you will be haunted for ever.

Singers and actors,
The stars we all see.
What of those who labour in the shadows,
Scientists and inventors. Creators of the world.

We see the fame we want to
The creators are hidden.
But performers show themselves,
Rulers of the stage.

We do not know the creator's name,
They do not perform.
Their performance is in their work.
Should they be known?

Eliza Ackland (12)
Alleyn's School

THE WEEKEND

The weekend has a slow beginning
I clumsily drift out of bed.
Then stumble down the stairs
Where the sofa is waiting for me.
And like a zombie I just stare
For a very familiar television
Has me under its spell.

Until the aroma of a frying egg
Lures me into my kitchen
Where I eat yet again.
Then I repeat my weekly ritual.
Of phoning yet another friend.

We meet a half an hour later
To muck around in the park
And then we make a decision
To which house should we return?

We usually pick my friend's house
But only because it's closer
And after our obsession
Of skating, footie and going a little crazy
We are tired and have a rest
With a glass of milk and a well-deserved TV
'Lunch!' is called from down below.

And we accelerate down a mountain of steps
To receive our precious treasure
Of cheese, tomato, a few spices and dough
Pizza soon fills an empty hole inside.

I repeat this every weekend
And you may think it's sad
But there is nothing wrong with being a little mad!

Alex Baddeley (12)
Alleyn's School

THE VAMPIRE

Soft and silent as a shadow,
She stalks the night without a sound.
The bare tree branches of October
Whisper and sway,
As if sensing an invisible presence.

She is disguised for this night,
All Hallows Eve.
The night where the undead walk free.
She could be a child in costume,
Or a dark princess of the night.

She stares at the moon,
Fangs glinting in the light.
She lifts her arms,
Draped sleeves rising like
Spidery bats wings.

Another figure slides
Out of the gloom,
His eyes are puddles of black ink,
Lips, red slashes in
The pale whiteness of his face.

Their eyes lock,
The princess and the prince
Together they slip
Into the shadows,
Seeking their prey
In the darkness.

Hannah Tottenham (13)
Alleyn's School

POEM

As the world goes soaring by
the pouring rain does not die
whipping my face
I find the place
flying above the human race.

Gliding high I touch the sky
diving low I touch the growth
twisting and turning flying free
a glint in my eye full of glee.

Swooping down the prey in my sight
the fat little mouse is quite light.

Suddenly there's a crack, a bang
plunging down the air sang
the wind whistling
the pain is high
I bid my soul goodbye
and as I lie in the bushy growth
my wings shudder, a hole in both.

The men come over
to find the bird dead
they laugh and sing
they shot in the wings and the head.

The four men stride away
for bad deeds done
will they ever pay?

Lawrence Rosenfeld (11)
Alleyn's School

THE TERRIFIC STORM

The clouds begin to build up force,
Preparing to open into a blinding storm.
As the clouds swirled over Mount Dirmon
The mountain realises its fate
And braces itself.
A cap of thunder sounds the start,
Followed swiftly by a bolt of lightning.
Rain steadily begins to fall,
Turning the snow-white blanket on Dirmon
Into a colourless, shapeless sludge.
The wind swirls harshly
And as the rain gains pace and power,
The mountain feels itself losing its grip.
The thunder now shakes the hills for far around
And the lightning begins to shatter the desolate land.
Hail now replaces rain
And provides a new white blanket,
For the now desolate and deserted countryside.
The lightning strikes again,
Shattering and crumbling the highest rocks,
Of the new surrendering mountain.
The thunder and lightning see their chance
And with one last roar and flash,
Destroy the peak of the mountain
Which crumbles hopelessly into the rest of the mountain.
A silence falls and the storm ceases.

Thomas Tyson (12)
Alleyn's School

WARNING!

When I am an old woman, I will ride a skateboard
And wear bikinis and do aqua-aerobics.
All my money will be spent on chocolate
And when I am bored I will go on holiday.

I shall trip people up with my walking stick
And eat all the sweets in the shop without buying them.

I will cook mouth-watering cakes and never share them
And sell over-priced sweets and clothes.

I will gamble and make bets for a living
And gatecrash parties
And always wear orange.

You can do mischievous things
And pretend that you are going mad
And eat whatever, whenever, however
Or just be a pain.

Until then, I'll act quite sensibly
And do nothing unexpected
Not show I'm age-affected
Act normal, undetected

But I'm experimenting already in secret
Because I want to be outrageous
When I am old
And start riding a skateboard.

Charlotte Bailey-Wood (11)
Alleyn's School

TEN LITTLE PIGLETS

Ten little piglets,
Sat drinking wine.
One got drunk
And then there were nine.

Nine little piglets,
Running a bit late.
One caught the bus
And then there were eight.

Eight little piglets,
Thinking about Heaven.
One dropped dead
And then there were seven.

Seven little piglets,
Picking up sticks.
One dropped the whole lot
And then there were six.

Six little piglets,
Going for a dive.
One floated away
And then there were five.

Five little piglets,
Picking gum off the floor.
One got stuck
And then there were four.

Four little piglets,
Climbing up a tree.
One fell off
And then there were three.

Three little piglets,
Trying to find a shoe.
One got bored
And then there were two.

Two little piglets,
Looking at the sun.
One went blind
And then there was one.

One little piglet,
Not having much fun.
One got sick
And then there was none.

Satish Jacob (12)
Alleyn's School

AUTUMN

The wind is calling,
The leaves are falling,
It is autumn once more.
Pitter-patter,
Pitter-patter,
As the rain hits the floor.
It is freezing
The weather is not pleasing,
Winter, summer and spring,
But in autumn
The wind is calling,
The leaves are falling
And that's all it will ever be.

Nicholas Edwards (11)
Alleyn's School

MIDNIGHT

The world of midnight is silent,
A flash lights up my room,
No sound however follows,
Objects around me seem to turn evil,
Shadows flicker and dance to create eerie symbols.

My curtains seem to move with no wind at all,
My desk turns to blazing red eyes to stare at me,
My books ripple as if cracking fingers.
My window shines a sickly green,
Creepers are all around me,
Trapping me in my own room.

A knife flickers in the half-light,
My fear tells me,
At least I am alive.

Babak Brazell (12)
Alleyn's School

THE AUTUMN

A rich, smoky smell heavy in the air,
Brown, yellow, red, green leaves hanging on the trees,
prickly green shells with a hidden treasure inside.
The night's getting earlier, morning getting later
Every day brings winter closer and every day a little colder
And new conkers and chestnuts to collect.
The gutters, littered with old leaves strewn everywhere,
Opening the prickly shell of a conker and finding a silky lining,
In the middle, a velvety soft conker.
Competitions at school for the biggest and best.

George Dolby
Alleyn's School

THE CAR BOOT SALE

People shouting, hustling, bustling,
Boots with no laces, happy faces.
Ancient oil lamps, worthless jewellery
And the smell of fast food fills the air.
Grandma's chipped china,
Mum's stripy tights,
Dad's old book, 'Nigella Bites'.
Grubby board games, pictureless frames,
Rows of soiled volumes, some without names.
Boxes of toys, not all for boys,
Headless Barbies, legless Kens.
Eyeless teddy bears sit and stare,
Sightless in the frosty air.
Will anybody buy me, does anybody care?

Charlotte Grace Bentley (11)
Alleyn's School

MAN'S BEST FRIEND

A dog is a man's best friend,
The wag of his tail and the lick from his tongue,
He is always around you, it is so much fun,
You walk him, he walks you,
He sometimes takes you to his friend called Sue.
You treat your dog when he is good,
Like every loving owner should.
When you wake up, your dog is on your bed,
Waiting eagerly to be fed.
Even when the weather is foggy,
You always have to walk your doggy,
A dog is a man's best friend.

Julia Thomas (12)
Alleyn's School

YEAR AFTER YEAR

Winter comes
And winter goes
And when it's here
There is plenty of snow.

Plenty of ice
And plenty of fun
But when it goes
Spring must come.

Spring does come
And spring does go
And when it's here
Flowers will grow.

Birds will sing
And bees will hum
But then it must go
And summer must come.

Summer comes
And summer goes
And when it's here
The sun will glow.

The sun will beat down
On robin and swallow
But then this will end
And autumn must follow.

Autumn comes
And autumn goes
And when it's here
The wind will blow.

Leaves will fall
Conkers will drop
Then this must end
And all must stop.

It will happen again
Year after year
Till the end of the world
Till all is clear.

Anton Baskerville (13)
Alleyn's School

WAR AND PEACE

There's always one dark spot on the horizon;
It resembles the people who seek help and safety.

There's always one light spot on the horizon
Which are not those millionaires out there who are rich and famous;
It's the people who have hope in their lives and those who
                                         never stop trying.

War pulls people apart;
It wrecks homes and lives,
Rips happiness into pieces and chucks hope down the drain.
War is caused by selfishness and hatred,
Not everyone has any hope in their hearts.

Peace brings people together;
It lightens people's hearts
And puts in a touch of love.

Why can't there be peace and love,
Friendship and kindness which spreads over the world.
Forget how different you are
And come together as one.

Peace won't go anywhere unless you fight for it!

Annabel Kenney (11)
Alleyn's School

THE TEST

Two weeks before the big test,
Alex was practising, trying to do his best.
Emotions running extremely high,
Blasting upwards into the sky,
Am I going to fail, am I going to die?
No, I'll pass just fine.

One week before the horror,
Revision falling like a tonne of bricks.
Work, work, it's the last week.
Must finish revision quick, quick, quick.
Am I going to fail, am I going to die?
Maybe I'll pass just fine.

Three weeks after the test,
Results were here at last.
The family's opening the letter
To find out that I'd passed!
Was I going to fail, was I going to die?
No, I was going to pass, just fine.

Alex Ooi (11)
Alleyn's School

CLARINET

She talks with me, in her own language,
Her voice is loud and clear,
It rings throughout the room and house,
So everyone may hear.

When I am gone, she stands alone,
The very last tree to fall,
Silent, cold and motionless,
Standing proud and tall.

She's long and thin and slightly shy,
She looks too harsh and cold.
But underneath, she's warm and friendly,
Not too hard to hold.

I care for her and keep her well
And clean and healthy too.
She comforts me, and sings to me,
Like all clarinets would do.

Jenny Bacon (12)
Alleyn's School

WINTER AND THE WOODS

Thunder grumbles, mercy colours stain the sky, clouds cascade
and the rain leaks out of the tumbling clouds.
I start precariously, I amble through the damp woods, mud squelching
and crisply-coloured leaves crackled underfoot.
The rain picks up and the pitter-patter on the canopy of leaves
is the orchestra of the drenched forest.
The wind whistles through the trees like a trapped spirit.
Shrubs are tipped with raindrops, just like arrows tipped with poison.
Holy penetrates the protection of my jeans and scars me like a knife.
The clouds cover the sun like a deep secret never to be told.
Berries, the fruit of the winter forest, dangle from their prickly home,
toadstools peek out from their rug of leaves and shrubs.
The end of the woods is nigh and the light peeps out from all sides,
The sky is as black as charnel, the wind begins to howl like tortured?
Out of the woods and into my house, I take off my soaked jacket
which trapped the cold out.
The flames of my fire licked me in, as I sat in front of it I realised
it was winter again.

Thomas White (12)
Alleyn's School

FRIENDS

The hand that wipes the tear away,
the words that promise faithfully to stay.
The laughter that is heard throughout,
this is what it's all about.

When you're lonely
or ready to give up,
they're there with advice and something to help;
(usually hot, steamy and in a cup).
The fooling, the jokes,
the time spent on the phone.
So in the end, you're never alone.

The make-overs
the clothes,
the shopping trips too.
It's a wonderful thing
what friendship can do.

Holly Terry (12)
Alleyn's School

YEAR SEVEN BIRTHDAY PARTY BLUES

I am caught up in a twilight zone,
Between the future and past,
I hope I can stay in both time zones,
With friendships that will last.

Do I invite the old friends?
Do I invite the new?
How do I know if I have any friends?
Tell me, what do I do?

What do I do if they don't get on?
What if they get in a fight?
I'm counting on you to tell me,
What do you think is right?

I want them to like each other,
I want them to all be friends
And want to see each other again,
When the party ends.

Theo Lee Ray (11)
Alleyn's School

MY SISTER

We used to be so close,
My sister and I;
Caring for one another,
Playing for the love of our mother.
But our love turned to dust,
Our friendship started to rust,
As the time flew by.

Our companionship corroded;
We were left with hate and fear,
Needling one another,
Fighting for the love of our mother,
Shedding many a tear.
But I hope our guns are unloaded,
So we can forget this deadly war
Then jealousy will be banished
And envy shall thrive no more.

Isabel Instone (12)
Alleyn's School

MY LIZARD

I have a lizard his name is Drax,
he sits on my shoulder and likes to relax.
He's colourful and spotty and likes to eat crickets
I give him calcium powder, to prevent him getting rickets.

His cage is a vivarium, it keeps him warm,
if he gets cold he'll turn very calm.
He's got wonderful vision, he can even see planes,
and sits at my window all day if it rains!

He likes to run, he's swift and fit,
but when he's tired he likes to sit.
He's good at climbing, he's strong and bold,
but he doesn't give a thought at what he's been told.

Then once came a time, a terrible day,
when we all thought Drax had run away.
We hunted for him through every room,
we thought poor Drax had met his *doom!*

But hooray, all the searching was in vain,
we soon had Drax sitting on my shoulder again.

Edmund Le Brun (12)
Alleyn's School

AUTUMN

Through the cold, dark woods I dash,
Trees surrounding me: oak, chestnut and ash.

Leaves of buttercup-yellow and cherry-red.
Spiral around me as I tread.

The tiny dewdrops soaking into my feet,
Showing autumn and winter are soon to meet.

No longer in-between my toes is the warm beach sand,
But above me are large flocks of birds migrating to warmer land.

Conkers from the bare-leaved trees are falling,
It won't be long before winter is calling.

Birds darting towards their nest,
Preparing for the long winter's rest.

Phoebe Taylor (12)
Alleyn's School

THE SOLDIER

I am a soldier, I live in fear of war
I stand up for my country
I walk for its safety
I fight for its freedom.

I stand in a trench which was built for this war
In my head bombs are dropping
Everyone is screaming
Panic is the only life
And yet, the world seems so silent
The enemy, they fire
My fellow soldiers, they move
Their faces hidden by masks
Masks of fear and hatred for those who wanted more
Another shot, another death
This war may end, but the fight for
Freedom will never end.

I am a soldier
I stand up for my country
I wait for its safety
I fight for its freedom.

Jessie Hemingway (12)
Alleyn's School

MARY AND JONAS' FORBIDDEN LOVE

A grey coloured galleon arrived in the port
With a thousand black slaves huddled on board
It was there that Mary Lineton
First set eyes upon Jonas, in chains
With the glint in his eye and a gold tooth smile
She chose him right away

And as he stood before her
She fell into a daze
She could not let her feelings show
For just a simple slave
So she sent him to the stables
To groom her horse's mane
As she walked into her bedroom her heart was all aflame

Oh Thomas, she wrote
Dear brother of mine, can I trust you with my word?
My heart has fallen for a penniless slave
Tell no one what you've heard

Thomas threatened Jonas with a gun to his head
Whilst secretly hiding the family ring
Underneath his bed
Then rode back home sniggering
Satisfied with his deed
Breaking his promise to Mary, desperate of his need

He told Mary what Jonas had done, stormed out and got his gun
As she ran into Jonas's arms, Thomas entered and shot
Mary jumped in front
Fearful, was she not

Dead, she lay on the floor
Dead, she lay all night
Betrayed by her own brother Thomas,
Weeping by her side.

Bella Audsley (11)
Alleyn's School

THE WAY WE ARE

When I was a tiny person
Sitting in my buggy
I used to watch the world go by
All around me were noises that I wanted to know about
The colours and flashing lights seemed like one picture

I remember being quite scared
All those people staring at me
All I could see was
Things on wheels, zooming past
Lego pieces built taller than the sky

Cold and warm, stuff called food
Sometimes I spat out what they put in
I might be small but I knew what I wanted
I didn't want to sleep when they said
There was far too much to do and see

I loved crawling around, laughing at anything
What people said I copied
But now I am grown up
I understand life, the way we live
A child's life is very precious.

Charlotte Sik (13)
Alleyn's School

PARTY PENGUINS

Penguins are so very cute
Waddling around in a black and white suit.
When under the water they swim and they glide
But when a leopard seal approaches, they run and hide.
Next the father goes looking for food
While he's gone they like to have a party dude.
Their eating habits are quite disgusting
Then they regurgitate it, how stomach busting.

They live in the most freezing atmosphere
Even so they never shed one tear.
Though they have wings they have always been flightless
It doesn't affect their total frightlessness.
Fast in the water and slow on the land
Their wings are firm, more so than a hand.
Their cries are music, better than any pop band
Locked up in a zoo with no ice, only sand.

The beauty of their habitat, of enchanted crystal
One million times the radiance of Bristol.
All penguins have day and night fever
The female specimens are the ultimate divas.
Just one of these beautiful birds of ice
Has a larger fan club than all the world's mice
Penguins really are the best Arctic friends,
They're cute, cuddly and round the bend.

Jack Oxley (11)
Alleyn's School

BAD FOR THE WORLD

The traffic is horrendous nowadays
It's noisy, stressful and bad for the world.
And if you get stuck in it
Oh, what a bother
Especially if you're late for school.

Imagine what it would be like,
If there were no cars, buses or taxis.
The calm open highways,
With a few horses and carriages,
Just trundling past.

The pollution is horrendous nowadays,
It's smelly, grey and bad for the world.
And if it gets any worse,
God help us all
Because the world could get too hot.

Imagine what it would be like
If there were no factories, petrol or acids.
The actual fresh air
Blowing strongly in your face,
As you walk down the path.

Nowadays,
Noisy, stressful, smelly and
Bad for the world!

Felix Mann (12)
Alleyn's School

GRANDMA

On that Sunday morning, I walked downstairs,
I knew something was wrong.
Many forlorn faces stared at me,
'What's happened?' I whispered to my mum,
'It's Grandma, Charles,' came the reply.
I knew instantly what had gone on during the night,
Grandma had gone to a better place.

It wasn't better for me though,
I never got to say how much I loved her.
I'd always told her I loved her, whenever she came round,
But I'd never said it passionately,
For she would always be around for me, tomorrow.
But that day it was different,
She wasn't there for me the next day, or the day after that,
To tell her how much I loved her.
If only I'd had a day's warning,
I would have kissed her and hugged her
And told her how much I loved her every minute of the day.

So I made a promise to myself,
To never let the sun set without an argument being resolved
And never to go to bed without telling my family that I loved them.
Even if I found myself disliking a member of my family,
I would tell them that I loved them.
For if I never saw them again
The last thing I would have said to them, would be,
'I really don't like you.'

I could never live like that

Charles Gallagher-Powell (13)
Alleyn's School

THE FISH WATCHER'S FIRST DIARY

Monday - to the seaside
Out there was a fin,
Heard a cheep, cheep, cheeping,
Think it was a . . . cricket.

Tuesday - to the pond
There was a boy with a fishing rod,
Looked and looked and there it was,
Think it was a . . . dolphin.

Wednesday - out at midday
Going for a sail,
Saw a big, big, biggy,
Think it was . . . cod.

Thursday - visited my fish bowl
Gave it a bit of food (fish wish)
It was hiding in its castle,
Think it was a . . . whale.

Friday - to the reservoir
There I saw a lark,
Suddenly a snap, snap, snapping,
Think it was a . . . goldfish.

Saturday - went down to the river
With me I took a meal,
Saw an electric, electric, electric.
Think it was a . . . shark

Sunday - tired of looking for fish
Made a bamboo wicket,
Asked some friends round, cadged a bat,
Had a game of . . . football.

Lily Peck (11)
Alleyn's School

THE STARS

Look up above and stop and stare
Enjoy the sights why don't you dare
Gaze at the stars in the air
Shining down on us over there

Bright and beautiful
Bold and brilliant

The stars, what a wonderful sight
Suspended above us in all their might
A long way away, at a great height
Further away than any kite
I'm bedazzled by all of this light
Because this isn't day - but night.

Ross Gill (13)
Alleyn's School

NATURE'S WILL

While eagles swoop
And hawks fly,
The jaguar runs,
The dolphins fly through the sea,
The animals gather,
In their masses,
To breed, die and eat.
The plants will grow,
The flowers will flourish
And thy nature's will be done.

Jack McCarthy (12)
Alleyn's School

THE CAGED BIRD

We call them pets, to love and to care,
But we turn a blind eye to what they have to bear.
To be kept every day, under lock and key
They are the prisoners, we the enemy.
So helpless and confined, and longing some day to be,
The caged bird has just one wish, a yearning to be free.
Enslaved in our power, living in invisible chains,
They crave to see the sun, to be refreshed by the rains.
Cage bars surrounding, suffocating their desire,
Dreams are fading, burning away like fire.
Mirages of hope, reflect a distant aim
To fly independently, wild and not tame.
So maybe there will be a time, many moons away
When the caged bird will be unknown, and fly liberated each day.

Emily Meins (13)
Alleyn's School

IN

In the universe, there's a galaxy.
In the galaxy, there's a Milky Way.
In the Milky Way, there's a solar system,
In the solar system, there's a planet.
On the planet, there's a continent,
In the continent, there's a war-torn country.
In the war-torn country, there's a province,
In the province, there's a village.
On the edge of the village, there's a shack,
In the shack, there's an old chair.
On the chair, there's a person sitting down,
In the person, there's hope for a future.

Christopher Mair (12)
Alleyn's School

I'M NOT A POET

I'm not a poet
You should know it
I cannot make a rhyme
I'm not a poet
You surely know it
My meter is a crime

I cannot get the vowels together
The verses don't make sense
I think I am condemned forever
To messing up my tense

I'm not a poet
You should know it
I cannot make a rhyme
I'm not a poet
You surely know it
My meter is a crime

I'd try to crack a single joke
But no one seemed to laugh
I used to mess up every time I spoke
And then look really daft

I'm not a poet
You should know it
I cannot make a rhyme
I'm not a poet
You surely know it
My meter is a crime

I've almost done my 30 lines
I can't believe I've done it
Wait a sec, I am a poet
Bet you didn't know it!

Alex Harvey (11)
Alleyn's School

THE ONION

The ugly onion glistened in the light,
With his hairy goatee well in sight.
His tough skin was peeling,
As I wondered what he was feeling.

Attacked by a knife,
As he rolled around in strife.
The old onion feeling lost,
As his life was losing its cost.

The onion was cunning,
When he sent us running.
For when the scent made the ladies cry,
We sent him into the fry!

Sizzling like oil in a pan,
We saw the old onion gaining a tan.
And it was soon
That we were eating him with a spoon.

Now I knew he'd gone for ever,
And that I would see him never.
How I remember the trouble that had gone on,
The old, hairy onion had gone.

Chris Peilow (12)
Alleyn's School

WHO IS IT THIS TIME?

Who is it this time that they're going to attack?
I'm not sure yet, but I think it's Iraq.
Why is peace the one thing we lack?
Maybe America is too busy watching its back.

Who is it this time that's going to feel the pain?
I am pretty sure that it's Saddam Hussein.
Is he the only person who is going to die?
No millions of other people will be left to lie.

Who is it this time that will be forced to hide?
It's all the people living in the Iraqi countryside.
Why should they be the victims of American pride,
When they don't even know who's on their side?

Who is it this time who is going to have the courage and dare
To stand up against Hussein and Bush - could it be Tony Blair?
It seems that victory is their only care,
But in war, how can winning *ever* be fair?

Joshua Alleway-Moger (12)
Alleyn's School

A WAR POEM

You can't imagine the longing of every
man in this war,

for the guns to go silent,
that I am sure.

'Go over the top and win the battle!'
that's what the officers said.

But they can't hear the screams
of the dying or see the rows of the dead.

So send us home to Blighty,
all you officers up high.

As home is better than Flanders -
we don't want to die.

Jonathan Berry (13)
Alleyn's School

WHAT IS YOUR HORROR?

Welcome to your nightmare,
I shall be your host,
Here you'll meet the darkness and frightening ghouls and ghosts.
Your biggest horrors will meet you,
Spiders, snakes and other creepy-crawlies too.
That is not all you shall see,
You shall also see vampires and zombies.
You are in a nightmare that you cannot escape,
Your biggest horror will meet you in the corner -
The person behind the cape.
Who is behind it? You shall have to wait and see,
So close your eyes and count to three.
Now look into the corner, who do you see?
He's your biggest horror,
He's small, he's nagging and he's your little brother.
He's your biggest horror.

Brian Wong (12)
Alleyn's School

SWIMMING

I stand beside the swimming pool,
I'm grinning like a chimp,
I just can't wait to get that feeling,
As I jump into the deep.
I take a running jump
And then I'm plunging through the blue,
I'm swimming like a turtle,
Like a whale, like a shark,
As the water rushes past me,
I dive into the dark,
My lungs are beginning to burst,
So I swim up to the top,
As I bob among the people,
I feel like a rock,
So I sink back down again,
To the deep murky blues,
As I start my little game again,
Just between me and you.

Angeli Jeyarajah (12)
Alleyn's School

IT'S CHRISTMAS TIME

The Christmas trees are all alight,
It's snowing till the world is white,
Santa's still one step away,
It's getting darker by the day.

Santa's workshop full of elves,
On their hats are little bells,
They're making presents for all of us,
They're making them from dawn till dusk.

The Christmas tree is all alight,
The decorations are so bright,
The branches are so thick and green,
This is all the Christmas scene.

Natalie Fiennes (11)
Alleyn's School

MY FAVOURITE PLACE

Far away in the forests of hope
Over the mountains of evil
My favourite place is in no place like these
But I bet you can't guess where it is.

Into the mines of gold
Out of pollution's reach
My favourite place is in no place like these
Perhaps you might guess where it is.

Up on the tallest of mountains
Under the deepest seas
My favourite place is in no place like these
I'm sure you will guess where it is.

My favourite place is a hundred years old
And one hundred and fifty feet tall
My favourite place is in no place like these
Now you shall know where it is.

My favourite place is in my very own house
Where I was born and bred
My favourite place is in no fancy place
But it's really my little bunk bed.

Hamish Hunter (11)
Alleyn's School

MY MUDDLED MIND

Oh no! I didn't do my homework today.
I've forgotten to learn the lines for the school play.

Why haven't those games I ordered, come yet?
The clothes I'd hung to dry, are still wet!

I'm gonna have lots of fun this vacation,
But I've still got to complete my geography presentation!

By mistake I've given myself a facial scar,
Oh my! I forgot to lock my dad's car.

I wonder who'll win The Champions League football?
Oh no! My science project is too small.

My mind is really muddled as you're seeing
That's why everyone calls me a confused being.

Yudhisthra Singh (9)
Alleyn's School

WHICH WOULD YOU CHOOSE?

I walk into a shop and see a really cool top,
I try it on and look at the price,
I gasp but think it's worth it,
because I look nice.

I move along and see a sign,
it says *Help a child, give money, be kind!*
I look at my top and at the price,
I could keep it for myself, or give a child a life.
I put that thought to the back of my head,
but can't help thinking about that child with no bed.
Which one would you choose?

Lucie O'Mara (13)
Alleyn's School

FOR THE LOVE OF HOCKEY

I love to play the game of hockey
Determination fired by the captain's armband
The whistle blows and the game fills your mind
In a different world altogether
A place where you forget all your sorrows
The feel of the stick gripped between your hands
A powerful extension to your arm
Energy surging and tension rising
Adrenaline rush as opponents are beaten
Supporters inspire that last bit of strength
Pulse racing as you dribble into the D
Total focus as the stick swings through the air
Padded up keeper, with a face full of fear
The ball cracks onto the backboard, raising a cheer.

Kit Hawkins (12)
Alleyn's School

IN THE TRENCHES

The sky turns dark and guns light the sky,
As soldiers fight on, only to die.
The lucky survivors try to sleep
But in no-man's-land, the wounded weep.
Silhouetted by the moon, the dead hang from the wire,
While safe behind the lines, officers sit round a fire,
Cold and hungry, men huddle in their trench,
Surrounded by corpses, rats and stench.
They think of hot dinners and of their homes,
And cry for their comrades, now cold flesh and bones.
They think of their wives and their next of kin,
Saying a prayer before the next battle begins.

William Chapman (14)
Alleyn's School

HELL

I sit in my funk hole
A tear in my eye
I remember my wife
As she kissed me goodbye
My helmet is dented
From shrapnel up high
What'll happen tomorrow
Will I live? Will I die?
The generals think that
They're all high and mighty
But all I want
Is to go back to old Blighty
The artillery stops
What! Is this the end?
No! Just the end of lives
Of the men that we'll send
They'll go over the top
And never come back
Oh why can't we change
Our plan of attack!
I'll remember these days as
My days of hell
That's if I return home
All safe and well.

Oliver Furber (13)
Alleyn's School

CUPID

The son of love,
Swoops like a dove,
Flapping his delicate wings.

A couple he spies,
One of whom cries,
His heart thumps with a shudder.

He pulls out his bow,
Which is never a foe,
Aims a beautiful arrow.

It soars through the sky,
He watches it fly
It enters a ruby-red heart.

He saw it in their eyes,
As true as the skies,
He knew that they were in love.

Their hands joined together,
Forever and ever,
Nothing could break them apart.

Mother of love
And father of war
The Cupid lives within us, forever more.

Vida Scannell (12)
Alleyn's School

OUR WORLD TODAY

Placed in the dark, deep, distance,
The sun, Apollo and his chariot,
Looks down on our humble Earth,
Like a giant to a child.

That child looks up,
Staring, a tear in his eye,
The sprinkled glitter amazes him,
Like nothing the bruised homeland can offer,
He spots the moon yawn.

Asleep, put to rest,
The ebony button blindly unaware,
All it knows is blue and green,
Not the familiar pain,
We see its sharp stare.

The jealousy, anger, hatred,
Sits tightly lodged in the bottom of every story,
Like a hedgehog in an unlit bonfire,
The violence, destruction,
Man-made, not prevented, tells each story.

Each story shows man's cruelty,
Not even Eve could show unselfishness.

Lottie Unwin (12)
Alleyn's School

SCHOOL

School is like a book,
Its pages and chapters are days and weeks,
Its ups and downs are lunchtimes and tests.
The climax is a report, may please, may not please
And the end, is another year gone.

Passed by in a couple of hundred pages
As ever, there is room for a sequel,
Another school year.
School is like a book, a book you may or may not
Like to read.

Maksim Mijovic (11)
Alleyn's School

THE GREEN DISEASE

It grows inside me like a disease,
spreading all over me, coursing through my veins,
Jealousy the king, over me it reigns.
I see people with special things which they've got,
I get this feeling, because I have not.
I try not to think of it, but when I take, along comes guilt.
People who are luckier than me, show me things
I would love to see,
But when it comes to saying goodbye, in the night
I grow green eyes.
I see people who are richer than me,
their lives are my dreams.
If only I could fly overseas, journey to another place,
get away from the rich human race.
But in the end, this is just a dream,
a dream of which I've grown so keen.
I hope one day I will be the same,
until that day I can only dream.
This is my life, a life in the dark, the feelings I have,
they push me to the edge, they're taking their toll,
they leave their mark on my tainted soul.
This terrible thing that grows inside of me,
it is bad, 'tis jealousy.

Max Hart-Walsh (11)
Alleyn's School

PEACE

An angel sent from Heaven
Carrying all the love from her heart,
Sending messages of peace
All over the vast land.

Every being falls quiet and calm
Content with harmony,
Feeling restful and happy,
Agreeing sensibly.

It may be hard to see
The meaning of peace,
For someone who has a heart of stone
But for others it is the best thing ever.

I know that soon everyone will see
The white dove with in its beak
The olive branch, the symbol of peace.

Hannah Waldegrave (11)
Alleyn's School

MY HALLOWE'EN

I was on duty in the guardroom
When a vampire appeared in the gloom
So I showed my tattoo
Of a man on the loo
And he took off his spooky costume.

I was drunk in the landlord's taproom
When a ghost offered me some perfume
I squirted shampoo
But he swore in Hindu
And today he is back in his tomb.

I was dancing in the duke's ballroom
When a werewolf charged in with a *boom*
I phoned the zoo
Whilst showering him with glue
But sadly he dragged me to my doom.

Freddie Smith (11)
Alleyn's School

VAMPIRE JUICE

Little eyes
Glare above the table.
Little hands
Clench
As she regards
The liquid
As though
It were an enemy
Come to poison her family.
It looks like the blood
That stained her skirt
When she grazed her knee.
She keeps her eyes
Fixed on that
Vampire's phial.
They move upwards
As her big sister
Enters, hair up, head bobbing
To her Walkman beat
And, grimacing,
Drinks down her glass
Of healthy tomato juice.

Chloë Courtney
Alleyn's School

TO BE ALONE

To be alone is . . .

Like the last leaf
On a bare, brown tree,
It's like the last gust of wind
In an ongoing storm.

To be alone is . . .

As peaceful as
A silent graveyard,
And as restful
As a bird in its feathers.

To be alone is . . .

Like one sad little star
Drifting calmly in the moonlight,
It's like a single flame
On a dripping candle.

To be alone is . . .

Like the last piece of food
In a cold, frosty freezer, waiting to be eaten,
It's like the world
Floating around in loneliness.

Hannah Ewens (12)
Alleyn's School

WRITE A POEM ABOUT ANYTHING

Write a poem about anything,
so many ideas to choose.
Write a poem about anything,
which to take and which to lose.
It's hard to think of anything
but there's a right one you must find.
When you first start looking,
they seem so far away,
But just look a little closer
and you'll find them any day.
I chose an easy subject,
one everyone knows about.
Write a poem about anything,
sounds easy but it packs a lot of clout.
Anything could be anything!
The sun, the moon, the rain.
Anything is everything,
happiness, sadness, pain.
All these subjects are so good,
but they never seem to work.
The words seem to hide away,
and in the shadows lurk.
So please teachers, I beg you
don't use that terrible phrase.
Write a poem about anything!
It could take days and days.

Hugo Jackson (14)
Alleyn's School

SANTA

Christmas carols on a rainy night
Santa Claus takes to flight,
His white beard flows in the midnight air
Delivering presents with love and care.

Rudolph the reindeer with a big red nose
Bright and shiny like a velvety rose
Eats the carrots that Santa gives
Lapland is the country where he lives.

I can hear bells, could that be Santa?
My heart starts to fizz like a can of Fanta
The door handle has started to twist
My room is suddenly filled with mist.

As my pressies are about to arrive
My night suddenly awakened and is alive!

Ben Chapman (12)
Alleyn's School

LIFE AT SCHOOL

Monday morning, start of a new week,
Miss with a new hairdo, a bold red streak
It's funny how teachers can do what they like,
But we're not allowed, not even a spike.

The rules are so strict, no smoking, no gum
It's work, work, work, more writing, more sums
Hand in your essay, hand in your coursework,
That's not the lot, she's handing out homework.

This week's gone by ever so slow
I've forgotten my textbook twice in a row.
I know I have to pay the penalty,
I'll be back for detention after biology.

Melissa Chan (11)
Alleyn's School

PASSING

The sun was scorching,
The crops on both sides were dry and dead;
The land was weary and drained from persecution.
The cries of poverty ascended to the heavens,
Accompanied by the rising dust from the disfigured, stony path.

A figure approached,
A woman in an old black hat with a drooping brim,
A black piece of thin net,
Attempting to cover the over-burdened pain,
And a tatty piece of black rag used as a dress.

She held the lifeless body of a little girl,
With a rope tied brutally around her innocent neck;
The mother embraced her daughter firmly,
She fell on her knees and wept,
Wept painful bitter tears, on her child's shoulder.

Which charm-talker could have read this sorrow,
This loss in her glass ball?
Who could undo this evil work of racism?

Is this a gypsy's life, thought the devastated mother?

Christina Lees (13)
Alleyn's School

D-I-S-C-O

On Friday . . .

The girls dressed up
And the boys dress down,
The girls wore a smile
And the boys wore a frown.
The DJ appealed to many in the crowd
The seats were all taken
So I sat on the ground

Everyone was shouting
And having fun,
The moon was up
And the sun was gone,
The lights were flashing,
The girls wore the crown
And after Kylie,
I was spinning around.

The night ended,
In an emotional way,
We all felt tired,
But I was okay,
It seemed like the end,
But there was more to come,
When they played
The Beach Boys - The Warmth of the Sun.

George Trickey (12)
Alleyn's School

YESTERDAY'S WEATHER

Yesterday the wind came,
Wuthering and winding from the west, gusting and galing,
Breaking and tearing apart the things in its way and rattling

the windows,
No chance to sleep.
Yesterday the wind came.

Yesterday the rain came,
Pattering gently at first on the panes, then harder,
Filling up leaf-blocked drains, flooding the gutters and the roads,
No chance to play, not yesterday.
Yesterday the rain came.

Yesterday the fog came,
Vanishing buildings, cars, people and street lamps,
In vain I stare out, wanting to see,
No chance to watch.
Yesterday the fog came.

Yesterday the snow came,
Eager children try to build snowmen,
But rush inside from the bitter cold with nose and toes frozen,
Roads are impassable with
No chance to drive.
Yesterday the snow came.

Yesterday the sun came,
With the tree leaves rustling gently
Making the air smell fresh
Lights go out and
Suddenly the streets are full of life,
Children play and kick and fight.
Let's drive and sleep and watch and play.
Yesterday the sun came.

Charlotte Anderson (11)
Alleyn's School

THE SONNET OF SONG

May I relate thee to a melody?
That weavest a sweet tune upon its score
A tune though divine, hath an impact short
But thine impressions is everlasting
Sometimes a perfect cadence blots the score
But thou'st do not decline or fall
Though harmonic, a melody must end
But thou shall forever play as sweetly
A melody can play on call only
Yet in my heart and mind, you play always
If just one play embodies a love
The heaven's orchestra could not hold mine
Forever shall our love's symphony play
Until the last minim of my last day.

Saffron Clague (13)
Alleyn's School

THE UNICORN

Shining silver in the moonlight
Almost glowing.
A milk-white mane
Soft and beautiful.
A single horn, dazzling and majestic.
The unicorn stood there
Silent and beautiful.

A sudden noise, a flash of light,
The clatter of hooves.
Into the darkness it sprang,
Gone forever.

Miranda Willis (11)
Alleyn's School

LIGHT

Every time I wake up something touches my eyes that can't be erased,
No bomb or destructive force can harm it,
When there is nothing but disease and despair all around,
it shines through.
You can't hurt it, but it can't hurt you.
So when darkness seems to fill the world, just remember,
Light is always there.

William Bedingfield (11)
Alleyn's School

POWERFUL

D   is for Damola who is kind and loving.
A   is for Africa where I come from.
M   is for my mum who is pretty and caring.
O   is for October when I wrote this poem.
L   is for the love the world should have.
A   is for the achievement that Damola hopes to get.

Damola George (11)
Bredinghurst School

LOVE IS GOOD

Love is the feeling when I am with Kelly.
Love is very inspiring.
Love is a good thing.
Love is very important.

Dominick George (12)
Bredinghurst School

MY THOUGHTS

B is for the beauty of black people.
L is for the love we have within.
A is for Africa.
C is for my culture.
K is for my kin who suffered and for kindness.

H is for the happiness we have inside us.
I is for intelligence which I have.
S is for sorrow.
T is for together which we have become.
O is for origin.
R is for roses falling off a tree.
Y is for years of slavery.

Mayo Makinde (12)
Bredinghurst School

LOVE IS . . .

Love is everything.
Love is happy.
Love is caring.
Love is helpful.

I think the world is loving
But sometimes spiteful.

Segun Bolodeoku (11)
Bredinghurst School

BREDINGHURST SCHOOL

B   is for breakfast before I go to school.
R   is for me as Ryan is my name.
E   is for the education that I get.
D   is for the nice dinner that I eat.
I   is for ICT that I enjoy.
N   is for the new teacher that came to our school.
G   is for the great time that we have.
H   is for HMS Belfast that I am going to visit.
U   is for how unkind people can be.
R   is for the roads that I use.
S   is for the staff who work so hard.
T   is for the time it took to write this!

Ryan O'Sullivan (12)
Bredinghurst School

MY FAVOURITE BONFIRE NIGHT

'The fireworks lasted a lifetime because
    I still remember them now'.

It was cold
But warm by the bonfire,
Which was bright and light
Bang, crack, pop and *whoosh*
The fireworks had started.
They smelled like boiled egg.
It was like watching a bursting box
Of crayons in the sky.

Kris Porter (13)
Bredinghurst School

I Wish . . .

I wish I was a millionaire.
I wish I never died.
I wish I was a king.
I wish I never cried.
I wish I was a football player.
But I am perfect as I am!

Leigh Smith (11)
Bredinghurst School

To My Girl

You are the sunshine in my life
And in my heart.
And when it rains in my heart
You are the umbrella that keeps my heart dry.
So let our love grow
Like cupid's arrow.

Joe Bhatia
Charlton School (SEN)

The One Girl I Need

The girl is sweet.
The girl is so hot.
Every time I see her, I melt.
If someone took her away from me,
I would die.

Michael Uwah (13)
Charlton School (SEN)

MY WHEELCHAIR

My wheelchair I like, it makes me feel safe and happy.
I can go to the shops, be pushed around
But sometimes I get wet and it makes me angry.
I also look at books on my tray.
I would love an electric wheelchair
So I can go around on my own.
Sometimes I sit in my big chair when I'm fed up,
It makes me feel happy.
I like coming out of my wheelchair and going on my bed.
My wheelchair is hard, cold and uncomfortable
And sometimes I get angry,
But I feel safe in it when I'm being pushed around.

Darren Lynch (14)
Charlton School (SEN)

WHAT IT'S LIKE TO BE IN MY WHEELCHAIR

It's good to be in my wheelchair
I go to parties and dance
I whizz in my wheelchair
But some people prance
Sometimes it's uncomfortable
I go to school in my wheelchair
And to the shops with Mum
My wheelchair makes me happy
It makes me want to hum
The doctor sees me
And looks after my knee
My chair takes me to parties at McDonald's
But you have to pay a fee.

Kayleigh Bennison (15)
Charlton School (SEN)

MY DAD

My daddy is a clever man
he is an ambulance man
he is very clever
my dad is a hero
Dad likes football
he likes his team, Man United.
My dad did not cuddle me when I was first born
because I was premature
but he cuddles me now.
Dad drives me in the car,
when we stop at the red light
he talks to me.
He used to be a cook
he works some shifts
I love him to bits.
Mum and Dad know me very well
Dad looks after me
so does my mum and my sister
I won't forget my baby sister.
When I have my tablet
if it won't go down
Mum or Dad give me chocolate from the fridge for me to eat.
Every time I go to the hospital
my dad will take me if he is off on a Monday.
Luke likes my dad.

Sam Beard (15)
Charlton School (SEN)

STANMORE

Stanmore is far, Stanmore is near.
It's OK, don't be scared, scared is OK, you will be fine.
Don't worry you will be fine.
The doctors are fine, you won't be lonely, you won't be sad.
The sun shines through your window.
You lay up and stare, you are going to be fine.
Anaesthetics are fit, sometimes fine.

Maria Whitefield (15)
Charlton School (SEN)

AUTUMN

Autumn is my Millwall sweatshirt
raining, we need umbrellas
wind turns them inside out.

Tommy Rogers (11)
Charlton School (SEN)

NEW HOME

As I stepped into my new home I felt like running away.
My old house was really nice, oh how I wanted to stay.
As I lay in my bed resting my aching head I can't help but think
Of all of the times I wasted watching TV.
Oh why, oh why I should have been saying goodbye.
Well I guess I'll have to settle down, I mustn't make a sound.
This place isn't so bad, it is really quite nice.
I've settled down now, can't you see,
This house is good enough for you and me.

Rhianna Crawford (11)
Chestnut Grove School

CELEBRATION POEM

Can you imagine the world around you
Just days going by one after the other
Not one day to be truly happy
Not one day to celebrate
Not one day where everyone gets together to rejoice
Not a reason for anyone to get along.

Think about Christmas and think about the feelings of everyone around
Some annoyed as they spend all their money
Some so excited they forget everything else around them
But when everyone gathers into one dining room
Or sit around a fire or tree
There's not one sad face
Not one lonely person
Now imagine it's gone, how do you feel?

Celebrations make the world around us
All different types smother us throughout the year
Some we celebrate and some we don't
There's one celebration that we should all recognise
Not Christmas, Hanukkah, Easter or Hallowe'en
We all celebrate the one day of the year
The one day that we were born
This celebration is celebrated by all.

Daniel West (13)
Chestnut Grove School

CELEBRATE ME

I'm da best, the one, DMD,
I've been around 3 years and a century,
I was brought up in a hip hop ground,
So all I know is a hip hop sound,
Sport and girls is what I've found,
I push my luck and go out of bound,

People say that I'm sometimes cruel,
But I dedicate it to my old primary school,
I go home and play some ball,
On the court, I look really tall,
But inside I feel really small,
But hey! My life is a celebrity hall.

Darrel Doyle (13)
Chestnut Grove School

GREASE

A dark carpet, a blanket, smothering everybody in the room.
Ice cold daggers stabbing at my throat, wounding me,
                              taking my breath away.
My face sweaty, everybody watching with intense power
Their eyes locked on me like a trained sniper.

The music starts, you can almost see the tension spreading
                              over the room.
You could cut it into pieces with one foul swoop of a knife.
Cold in my throat but boiling all over, scolding me.
My eyes watering, my eyelids wanting to shut but not being able to.

The light on me, shrouding my face, making me feel sick.
I can only see the front row, the rest lie in mystery.
Everything silent apart from me and the music.
My legs knocking as I try to keep them apart.
My heart dancing in circles, rushing my chest.

Finally it's finished, my body stops being tense.
Relief seeps through my body, unclouding my head.
There is a roar of claps and whistles.
A smile finds it way onto my face.
Finally I have finished it.

Oscar Brazil (13)
Chestnut Grove School

CELEBRATIONS

Warm welcomes into a disco lit room,
I noticed the very smartly dressed groom.
Family and friends were everywhere in sight,
My eyes dazzled because the disco ball was so bright.
Exotic foods of every choice
I began to head that way but was stopped by a voice.
Her big white dress and her hair curled and tied,
Everyone shouted, 'Hooray for the bride.'
My eyes returned to the food,
I was in a very hungry mood.
The bride pulled me, I nearly slipped on the floor
And realised we were heading to the door.
We came out into the street
And I knew I'd never be able to eat.
Some music came on and the bride began to groove
She beckoned me onto the spotlight to do a move.
My eyes fell onto a group in the corner playing, the band
Luckily the groom came and held the bride's hand.
I slipped through the crowd slowly,
All was left was some cold ravioli.

Abigail Wighton (14)
Chestnut Grove School

SURPRISED

As I walked through the door
I saw balloons, food and a lot of bright lights.
It was my party,
I was so surprised!

I was welcomed into my house with a shout 'Surprise!'
From my friends and family.
I would not move, I could not move,
I was so surprised!

I walked around, there were presents, balloons, poppers,
Family I hadn't seen in years
And a huge cake,
I was so surprised!

I could not believe my eyes
Most of these people ignore me
But this was my party, one of the best,
I was so surprised!

Stuart Watkinson (13)
Chestnut Grove School

HER WEDDING DAY

With just a week before the biggest day of their lives, family
and friends rush around to get everything sorted within five days.
With Mum and Dad sorting out all of the decorations and food,
brother and sisters, also friends getting a place for the day
and setting the room up with decorations,
while she just goes out shopping for her dress.
On the other hand her fiancé is looking for somewhere nice
for their honeymoon, stressing himself.
Nearly everything is done in three days
but there is still invites to be done, with the time of 24 hours.
Once the dress is bought her hair and make-up is to be decided.
On the day her mum, sisters and herself wake up 2 hours before
everyone else to get her hair and make-up done and out of the way.
On the way to the church she is really nervous and starts to cry
but she recovers when they reach the church.
This is the moment everyone has waited for,
the moment where someone close to them gets married
to the man of her dreams. The love of her life,
but most of all she loves him and this is her wedding day.

Verneece Hilaire (13)
Chestnut Grove School

WINNING THE LOTTERY

I slowly turned on the TV, clutching the ticket,
The programme had just started,
The machine began to roll,
I was fully concentrated on the small screen
The first number took forever to come out,
It was a green ball,
I was hoping it was on my ticket,
I had memorised the number on my ticket,
The first number to come out of the machine was on it.
But I still needed 5 more numbers to win.
Then the second number dropped,
I hadn't blinked since the first number,
But I didn't care because the second number was on my ticket,
Sweat trickled down my face
And my heart was beating a million times a second,
There was a tiny chance I could win this,
I ran as fast as I could to get a drink to calm me down,
But by the time I came back the third and fourth numbers had appeared,
I prayed that they were on my ticket, and they were,
My heart rate was off the scales and I wanted to scream with joy,
But there were still two numbers to go,
The fifth number rolled out,
Everything seemed to be in slow motion,
Then the TV went fuzzy and I was on the verge of tears,
I hit the TV as hard as I could, and surprisingly it worked,
The fifth number was on my ticket,
I had already won a lot of money, but I wanted all the money.
Then the final number rolled down,
I was dreaming of things to buy with my money, if I won,
Then the number was revealed,
I turned around where a faint voice said,
'Santhokie, time for school.'

Santhokie Nagulendran
Chestnut Grove School

CELEBRATION

People were happy, people were laughing,
The multicoloured lights blazed through the dark party hall,
Merry people toasted with their fine wine,
The finger buffet food was simply sublime,
Dancing and singing all night long,
Singing their cheerful and happy song,
Never in the street was a party so lively,
There and then a magical night.

The morning after was a horrible sight,
It took an awful might,
To clear up the junk, cups and wrappers,
It seemed a while to be finished,
But hours later it was completed.

Zainab Kauroo (13)
Chestnut Grove School

THE 11TH HOUR

Shelly's 11th birthday was here at last,
She invited friends for a birthday blast,
They arrived at one,
For lots of party fun,
They found a banquet lay,
A magical display
And in the middle, a giant jelly,
It's in the shape of Shelly,
'But no food for now,' Shelly did say,
'Because today of all days is my day,
And I say no food for you will devour,
Until the later time of the 11th hour.'

Amy Mutch (13)
Chestnut Grove School

LOVE AT FIRST SIGHT

When I first saw her, she turned away
I tried to chat her up, she had nothing to say.
I couldn't give her up, she was the girl that I need.
It was like she was the soil, I was the seed.
She got to know me, she thought I was alright.
When she was with other boys I couldn't let her out of my sight.
When I looked in her eyes, it was like the deep blue sea
I remembered the day she said she loved me.
I said to her that I felt the same.
I was 13, she said that's a shame,
Because she was 15 and in her prime
Sexy girl, I want you mine
You and me together that would be a dream.
I think we could make a first class team.
You were the brightest girl I had ever seen in my life
I wanted you to become my wife.

Daniel Gurney (13)
Chestnut Grove School

LIFE IS WORTH LIVING

Countless babies are born every minute,
Some big, some small, some fat, some thin,
Whatever they are, life is worth living,
Stop the grieving, start the believing!

Celebrate while you're here on Earth,
Make the most of it before it ends.
If you've sat there sad and drooping,
Get up now, it's a new season!

Many lives have been taken away,
But you have to move on anyway,
Whatever happens, life is worth living,
Stop the grieving, start the believing!

Johanne Williams (12)
Chestnut Grove School

IN MY HEAD

Other people celebrate,
with gifts, food and wine,
but I have my celebrations
in my tiny little mind.

You see I have no one,
to celebrate with, no friends or family,
but I remember when I did
and that is what I celebrate.

In my head I have
gifts, champagne and music,
I get drunk and have a laugh,
and dance the whole night through.
And in my head I have famous people
dead or alive.
Because in my head it doesn't matter,
no one else can see them, just me.

But sometimes I see people laughing at me,
sitting by myself,
but I don't care,
I've got my head
and nothing else matters to me.

Gemma Tester (13)
Chestnut Grove School

BIRTHDAY CELEBRATIONS

There was a rush of cold blood
and goosebumps up my legs
I was so excited
I thought I was dead.

I woke up in the morning
and saw all the presents
I was going to open them
but my mum said, 'Don't you dare.'

There was a smell of candles
strawberries I think,
party poppers and balloons
with booze in the sink.

Everyone started singing
as the cake followed in
my mum tripped over
and it fell in the bin.

Everyone was laughing
it was quite a celebration
my nan got drunk
luckily it was her vacation.

The day was over
everyone went home,
the next day had come
and my birthday was gone.

Shantelle Collins (13)
Chestnut Grove School

I'M NOT SURE

I'm not sure,
Is there a cure,
For someone who's not sure?

I don't know,
Please don't let the answer be no,
I hope there is a cure,
For someone who's not sure.

Am I right?
Is this something I should write,
I hope there is a cure,
For someone who's not sure.

Is this wrong?
It doesn't know like a song,
Or ring like a gong.

Is this a fight?
I hope I am not right,
I will get smashed in the face
And thrown all over the place!

Am I in love?
With someone like a dove,
Who's like a baby in a cradle,
Or maybe he is just an angel.

Oh! I'm not sure,
Is there a cure
For someone who's not sure?

Charelle Christian (12)
Chestnut Grove School

A NEW BABY?

I just took the test
That will tell my destiny
Am I a mother?
Soon to be?
Will I be happy?
Will I be sad?
Are the results
Good or bad?

The seconds are minutes,
Minutes are hours,
Stuck in this small cubicle,
Thinking of flowers.
Boy or girl,
The only thing the test won't tell.
Blue or red?
The only thing running through my head.

Blue, blue, the test is blue!
I'm having a baby!
Do I want a baby!
Yes, yes, a baby for me,
Something small to comfort me!
What will it be!
Sadie if a girl, Jack if a boy,
Huge cuddly teddies for it's only a toy.

'Well,' I say, to Sadie or Jack, 'be gentle.
Try not to hurt my back!'
'For I am so happy, I will have a party,
I shall have to tell Marty, he's your dad.'
To him, the news could be bad,
But this was my baby, and it shall live
A long happy life, just Marty, me and my baby.

Zirena Walker (13)
Chestnut Grove School

PARTY

Clink goes the glasses
as bubbles fly in the air

I place the glass
upon my lips.

I feel a chill of bubbles
go down my spine.

The last cream whipped cake
on the silver plate.

With the torment of
sheer delight.

And without hesitation
I take a bite.

Alissa Abena (13)
Chestnut Grove School

CELEBRATION

C   is for getting a cat,
E   is for being excited,
L   is for having good lyrics,
E   is for being eventful,
B   is for being beautiful,
R   is for getting a rabbit,
A   is for being accomplished,
T   is for being tame,
I   is for being inspiring,
O   is for being orderly,
N   is for being born in November.

Katherine Drake (12)
Chestnut Grove School

A CELEBRATION OF SECOND THOUGHTS

Almost ready to give birth
She walks down the corridors looking at the newborn babies,
As she hears them cry, she looks at the young ladies.
Girls as young as sixteen had just given birth,
Whilst others regretted it and said their babies were the most
                    ugly things on Earth.
She looked in horror as tears rolled down her face,
Then she said to herself, look at them; they are so young, what a waste.
Moving swiftly down the corridor, she begins to feel pains,
Slowing down her pace she begins to strain.
As she sits down on the cold hospital floor
Wondering who will be the next person to come through the door.
She thinks about life before she became pregnant,
Did she really want to bring a child into this world
If she was not prepared?
As she thought carefully she wasn't aware,
Her family were watching her through the window.
Gripping onto her husband's hands, she screamed,
The pain was unbelievable,
As the baby slowly became visible she smiled.
She thought carefully and laughed, and said she was proud,
                    her child was born
And toasted to 'My second thoughts'.

Ruth N'Choh (13)
Chestnut Grove School

THE END

As I stood on the hard, wet concrete
Waiting for him to come home from the war,
I wondered if he would ever make it back at all.
He'd been carted away to battle 3 years and 100 days ago
To fight the Germans off for good,
I still didn't know whether he was alive or not.

Train after train, carriage after grubby carriage arrived
But there was no sign of him.
I saw hopeful mothers have their hopes shattered
By husbands and sons not showing up
Which caused them to bury their heads into handkerchiefs.
I was sweating with fright and anxiety
As the last train rolled into Platform 4. This must be him.
He has to be on this one.

The steam cleared and a dark silhouette appeared.
There was a filthy man
With a duffel bag slumped over his shoulder.
It was Dad! My distress cleared, relief replaced it.
I hadn't seen him in 3 years and 100 days!
I raced up to hug him, tears welling up in my eyes,
Celebration fireworks exploded in my mind.
As we held hands, walking home, I knew it was *the end.*

James Armian (13)
Chestnut Grove School

THE MOMENT

The moment had struck me
Time held still,
Silence dawned over the horizon
To sunk my eyes
Within the galaxy swirl of stars
They shone like
The purest diamonds more than
The precious golds of the universe.

The heart within one
Thumped the sound of a percussion,
The blood tickled down my spine,
Thrilling me with the feeling
Of endless joy.
The flame alight in my heart
Named in a moment of stillness.

A crystal clear blue sky,
Gleamed beyond -
Fluffy silver clouds through my head,
The gateway to Heaven opened.
Sound of sweet music had echoed
Across the sky, softly playing.
The sight of death? or Love's dream?
Love is blind.

Samina Bhatti (13)
Chestnut Grove School

CELEBRATION

Heart thumping when someone walks by,
He doesn't know how I feel,
When he comes I act all shy,
What a feeling, what a life.

There isn't a day that goes past,
That I think, 'is this love gonna last?'
My love for you is like a dream come true,
Every night I dream of you.

Every time I hear your name,
I think I'm going insane,
E- - - - -,
That name was made for me!

Will this celebration of love forever last?
But I will never know unless I act fast.

Why has this happened to me?
I do not know,
If you knew how I felt,
Then you would know.

Is it love or is it me?
I think this is love,
Which was meant to be.

Elicia Gayle Bouncer (14)
Chestnut Grove School

CELEBRATION

Packed my bags, off I go
Searching far, for a place, I wish to live.
Not knowing where, where I shall live
Not knowing how, how I will ever begin.

Nice little area, quiet and sweet
Getting rid, rid of all my bitter sins.
I've found my spot, so I unpack and settle down.

Now looking back, I think to myself
Was my past so bad to leave?
Was it so bad I got up to leave?

Whether it was or wasn't, I've left now.
No looking back, no moving on.
I stay put and celebrate my joyful new home.

Sezin Taner (14)
Chestnut Grove School

THE RACE

They all line up to race, they wait and there's old number 1
In the lead, he's in anticipation of winning,
Number 3 is catching up,
Oh no, he fell over and there's going to be a clear winner,
Number 7.

Number 7 walks up to get his award,
Hey that's not fair, he used a horse
But no one said which race it was.

Andrew Webber (12)
Chestnut Grove School

DEATH

Sometimes is too far away to think about it
Sometimes is too close to do something
But one day it will come to you
On that day you'll feel awful you'll feel blue
Breathing slowly, blinking slowly
Watching your life as a film in your mind
A film that only shows your special bits
In seconds you'll be gone
You'll finally have peace
Everyone will leave you alone
You'll notice that
Yesterday everything was happiness
Today everything is sadness.

Ana Almeida (14)
Chestnut Grove School

THE NIGHT BEFORE CHRISTMAS

I came downstairs to see a glorious meal,
Turkey, stuffing, roast, brown, shiny potatoes and
                              delicious creamy gravy.
I had to wait because it was time to open one present
                              before Christmas Day.
I opened the present with delight, carefully unwrapping
The sparkling red wrapping,
To find it was a hand-knitted, thick, beige scarf
With my initials in black,
I was gobsmacked, I picked it up and swang it
Round my neck with joy.
Then I jumped up and hugged my mum tightly.

Jade Llewellyn (11)
Chestnut Grove School

To Celebrate

To understand the meaning of our lives,
To love and care for one another,
To be together forever,
To celebrate our lives,
The way we live and love,
Not to hate but to care.
To smile and laugh with your friends,
To be together,
To help each other and never hate your friends,
Celebrate, celebrate our lives,
Celebrate your happiness and
Friendships with your friends,
To celebrate your dreams that
May even come true,
Just celebrate with me!

Ieva Adomaviciute (12)
Chestnut Grove School

Christmas

Christmas is a time for family
To get together,
Eating hot food, a big turkey
On the beautiful table,
The whole house is sparkling
With decorations,
Having fun and opening presents.

Ismel Boateng
Chestnut Grove School

PARTY

Excitement, joy, clatter, racket,
Blasting music, I just can't hack it,
Balloon, clowns falling down,
Running, jumping,
Screaming, shouting,
She's walking, talking,
The ultimate party girl.

Crowds of young and old,
Have joined the party,
Dressed in gold,
Dancing, prancing, full of fun,
After the party they all run,
Then the party was done.

Ayesha Amaka (14)
Chestnut Grove School

MY NEW BROTHER

N   is for new beginning,
E   is for excitement,
W   is for watching him grow.

B   is for new baby boy,
A   is for attending his birthday,
B   is for being there for him,
Y   is for a little youngster.

Larisha Dixon-Brown (12)
Chestnut Grove School

A DREAM I WANT TO COME TRUE

I have a dream,
A dream to change the future,
Make it what it doesn't seem,
To make the world a better place,
If I could stop all the wars,
It would make me want to hug you.
I could go back in the past,
I would celebrate my life at every chance I have,
Stop Hitler from killing the Jews,
No one to order,
No one to cook our stews.
I would save the Twin Towers,
Save everyone from the disasters we cause,
Make the world a better place,
To make the future a nice future,
Make my dream come true.

Sophia Attias (13)
Chestnut Grove School

BEINGS

People are so totally cruel,
Making the animals lives dull,
They don't care about them a bit,
All they want is their meat.
They treat them as if they have no feelings
And don't care about the killings,
Being squashed together in cages,
Tighter than the magazine pages,
They look at life go by,
Just waiting, waiting to die.

Marika Kulesza (12)
Chestnut Grove School

MARRIAGE

People gather in celebration of life,
The commitment of creatures like husband and wife.
The bells in the chapel ring clear and loud,
While the happy couple stand tall and proud,
What thoughts are going through the groom's mind?

What if he hadn't walked out of his door?
What if he'd taken the lift to the bottom floor?
Then where would he be on this day?
Would be he painting his flat grey?

The groom takes a sudden gasp of relief,
So happy he'd met his wife Clarice
For him this day would last forever
And that's how long they would be together.

Hannah Evans (11)
Chestnut Grove School

CELEBRATION

Celebrations are the good times standing on the podium
After winning first place.
Getting hyper then getting more excited, stunned
All mixed in one.
Happy then ever shocked to be first place,
Laughing and joking to be first place.
Looking around out my awards stunned,
And amazed to be like this.
Running around the track stunned to be first place
Just won the race, stunned and amazed.
Looking at the crowd roaring so loud.

Danny Hewett (12)
Chestnut Grove School

Birthday Poem

It's my birthday
It's my birthday
All the celebrations

It's my birthday
It's my birthday
All the sweet presents

It's my birthday
It's my birthday
All the great friends

It's my birthday
It's my birthday
All the great fun.

Chike Blagrove (12)
Chestnut Grove School

Fireworks

Fireworks are full of light,
Which is also good at night,
Children, adults come to see
When I hear a big bang it really scares me.
Many colours in the sky,
Looking up it seems so high,
Little children screaming loud,
Can't hear anything in the crowd.
Time for take-off, here it goes,
Now we can watch and see it explode.

Clinton Harrison (11)
Chestnut Grove School

PLUS 1

Every year you're plus 1,
This means love,
Not hatred.

Every year you're plus 1,
This means life,
Not death.

Every year you're plus 1,
This means older,
Not younger.

Every year you're plus 1,
This means,
You,
Your birthday,
Your life and
Getting older.

Paulo Gouveia (12)
Chestnut Grove School

NEW LIFE

N   ow I am starting to grow,
E   at my food and drink my drinks,
W   orld is all mine.

L   oving and caring come so easy,
I   njured makes me cry,
F   resh new start,
E   xploring the world is only a dream.

Zulal Okuyucu (12)
Chestnut Grove School

GOODBYE MY FRIEND

The sun punched his way through the dark angry clouds.
It was time for the funeral,
The day began.

We finally reached,
His face was white like snow, he felt like he was wearing
A rubber mask.

His sleeping bed that was what I called it,
It looked antique,
Also luxurious, we had excellent workmanship with
The craftsman.
It felt smooth and looked shiny
And very hard.

I felt unhappy
And everyone was tearful,
Sympathetic to us and sluggish like I was.

People felt empty and hopeless,
Angry and let down but
Remembered him how he was.

We went to the pit as I called it,
Because I was five.
The pit dark, gloomy
It was black as soot,
I picked up a piece of mud
It was brown and hard as a tree bark.

Javean Miller (12)
Chestnut Grove School

GHOULS' NIGHT

All is silent on this night of nights
When the trees sway without the wind
And phantoms spring from every corner
Dancing in the dark
And the Devil's flame breaks from its inferno of a jail
Setting the Earth alight.
Zombies walking, witches cackling
Sending a chill through the Earth.
Mayhem lives on this night of nights
Where witches howl and werewolves fight,
So beware on this night of nights
You may just die of sudden fright.
For this is ghouls' night.

Latifù Mumuni (11)
Chestnut Grove School

CARNIVAL

C   rowds start to gather in the square,
A   romas of food float on in the air,
R   hythms of music long into the night,
N   obody sleeps till the first morning light,
I   ngenious inventions to wear and more,
V   ibrant colours of costumes galore,
A   tmosphere charged with excitement and fun,
L   aughter and cheering the carnival's begun.

Michael Huseyin (14)
Chestnut Grove School

CELEBRATIONS

I've got to go now,
I tidy up my hair,
I think that I am moving,
But I just stand and stare,
It's time to go now,
I must decide,
Whether to wear my hair up,
Or wear it to the side.
I need to get my dress,
But my room is a mess.
I've got to go
To put on a show.
My room is still in a state,
But importantly I must not be late.

Rochelle De-Terville (12)
Chestnut Grove School

LOOK AT THAT FOOL

His dribbling with the ball,
Look at that fool,
Bang he shoots,
There goes his boots,
Hits the goalie's head,
Now he's dead,
Boo! Goes the crowd,
The footballer is proud?

Leigh Richards (12)
Chestnut Grove School

THE TEST

Tick-tock, tick-tock,
This clock is driving me mad,
I'm only on the first question,
I know I'm doing bad,
How are you doing? Are you doing OK?
There's ten minutes to go,
Hip hip hooray,
Phew, I've finally finished,
Only seconds to go,
Will I get a 6+, I just don't know!

Lamara Amy Forder (12)
Chestnut Grove School

MY CHESTNUT TREE

My chestnut tree
Standing young and strong
It brings back memories of things that are gone
Members of family, I didn't know for long.

My dad is dead now
But as a symbol of him we planted a tree
It helps give good memories
Back to me.

The tree is still young
8 years old
But it is a strong tree
And it will hold.

Owen Kinsella (11)
Dulwich College

THE BRANCHING TWISTING WILLOW

The willow is young, twisting and turning in the free space.
It is sprouting its first branches and vine.
It is growing higher and higher to the clouds,
Like an eagle majestically soaring up into the air.

The willow has now grown stronger, tough like a rhino,
Its vines begin to grow leaves,
It is growing into other gardens,
Its trunk is thick like a stone.

Now it is summer and the willow is at its prime,
Once again flying high into the sky.
Becoming stronger, larger and growing even stronger vines,
It is slightly windy and the vines are whistling and
Swaying in the cold night air.

It has now come to the winter where the willow will freeze,
It will also be stripped naked of its leaves,
It is icy making it hard to grow anymore,
The wind is chillier than ever and the tree is rustling in the late night air.

It is now spring and the willow feels reborn,
It is growing its leaves back once again happily growing
Stronger and bigger.
Other plants can be seen growing around it,
It is now growing old as it lives its long life.

It is now again summer back where it all started,
The willow is now old,
Growing slower than ever in its entire life,
The tree is still happy though eagerly waiting for the new cycle.

Richard Pagliuca (11)
Dulwich College

APPLE TREE

Apple tree, apple tree,
How every year
You repeat your eventful cycle . . .

In spring your dazzling white blossom,
Your reputation grows of being,
The most colourful tree in the whole area,
At the end of spring you start to loose your snow-white blossom,
But you don't go into a dark alley waiting for next spring,
You start to grow juicy apples for your owners to eat.

During the summer you watch all the flowers at the back in full colour,
Whilst you are growing your fruit only 6 feet above the ground,
You wait your turn ready to stun the area again by your
Succulent apples,
It is a shame that your fruit is not ready to eat in mid-June,
When the scorching heat blisters your skin and your throat swells up
Wouldn't go a miss.

But it is worth waiting for in the autumn, the days are short,
You provide us with tarts and sumptuous apples on their own for
Afternoon tea.
But when you are most thanked for is when the days are freezing
And we have apples for puddings in pies, crumbles, stuffed with sugar
And sultanas with hot custard.

After Christmas when the celebrations are wearing thin,
We look outside and say in our heads,
Apple tree, apple tree,
How every year,
You repeat your eventful cycle . . .

James Lawlor (11)
Dulwich College

113

AUTUMN

Autumn leaves are falling,
Very thick and fast,
I can hear the wind calling,
While the summer no longer lasts.

Winter is near,
It's bringing the cold along,
Autumn is here,
Threatening winter three months long.

September to November,
Is all dead and brown,
No more heat just brrr,
As temperature goes down.

But a good thing about this season,
That conkers are beginning to drop
And for a very good reason,
Conkers will now be going pop.

Also on October's last day,
Is a very frightening time,
When the sun is kept at bay,
Hallowe'en is here on the midnight chime.

Autumn leaves are falling,
Very thick and fast,
I can hear the wind calling,
While summer no longer lasts.

Philip Parbury (12)
Dulwich College

NATURE'S MYSTERIES

As a wild stallion runs,
Across the African plains,
As a dolphin glides through,
The seas,
You and I breathe.

As a kangaroo,
Leaps across the bush,
As the eagle hides in the air,
We watch and stare.

Now to night the
Animals change,
A squeak,
An eerie noise.

The owl that hoots,
When we sleep,
The bats that screech,
The ravens that soar
Restless in the London Tower
We hear.

The fireflies, the stars
Of the Earth
Their lights everlasting.
The trees are still
Like fossils trapped in time's
Mighty cage.

As their shadows create a vortex
Of darkness,
This marvel
Beyond the imagination and
Knowledge.

Ankush Patel (11)
Dulwich College

THE COLD HEART OF SLAVERY

A dull dark day settles upon England
Men and women walk heads down
The rain splashes and patters on roofs
These men and women wish not to be outside
But it's the master's will, not theirs

People ignored them
People whipped them
Sold them then worked them to the gate of death
Still they had to get up the next morning

A whip slaps on their hands
A whip lashes over their behinds
Yet they do not shake or cry
But try to work harder and faster
Their faces worn with pain
Their hearts scarred with rage

Who are these poor ones?
Those who have no will
Except to serve those who ill treat and beat them
Who are these who work in all weather?
But still feel the straps of leather
Who are these treated like dirt?
Even the dogs get fed better

So you tell me straight to my face
Are these our brothers
Or
Slaves.

Michael Okocha (12)
Dulwich College

TREES

They're always there,
No matter where.
Forever merry,
The flowering cherry.

In spring they're green,
Some tall, some lean.
Some ugly, some fine.
Some majestic, like pine.

When the sun is strong,
The shadows are long.
The branches will reach
From the sturdy beech.

To the cool days ahead,
The leaves go to bed.
With a wonderful pillow,
From the elegant willow.

Lit by a glow,
Of wintertime snow.
Red berries how jolly,
From the Christmas time holly.

And after the cheer,
We start a new year.
So everyone sees,
The wonder of the trees.

Christopher Cudd (11)
Dulwich College

THE BOY AND HIS OWL

A boy went into a forest,
He wanted to get away from the world,
He wanted to think.

His mind soared,
He went into different worlds and times,
He heard a distant screech
He turned around.

The eyes were like great balls of fire,
Superior lights to the sun and moon,
They made the boy uncomfortable.

The boy ran,
The owl did not chase him,
But just stood there and watched.
Waiting.

Left to itself the owl stood still as a rock,
As if daring any creature to step forth into its territory,
But what the owl didn't know was that something,
Something unusual was slowly coming up behind it.

James Oyedele (11)
Dulwich College

WHEN AUTUMN COMES

It gets darker sooner,
Each day it gets colder,
But saddest of all,
The leaves begin to fall.

The trees are laid bare,
As if to declare,
That summer has ceased
And the sun has been released.

If only it would snow
And the wind wouldn't blow,
Then winter would be okay,
If only it lasted one day.

Henry Foreman (11)
Dulwich College

THAT'S MY TREE!

It stands there alone, in the autumn air,
Its golden brown branches left utterly bare,
I look up at this great tree
And wonder if it was me,
How it lasted till this day,
From the ice-cold to the sun's rays,
That's my tree!

As the leaves fall to the ground,
Piling up into a big mound,
I am playing,
The tops of the trees are swaying,
Above the trees sings a lark,
Then comes the approaching dark.
That's my tree.

The leaves are crunching under my feet,
Waiting for the summer's heart,
The birds are starting to fly away,
Not standing the colder days,
I will always be there for my tree,
Until there is no more of me.
That's my tree.

Arif Hossain (11)
Dulwich College

WINTER HAS COME

Plum trees,
Apple trees,
Standing on the lawn.
The sweetest of nectars
Swaying in the wind.
Menacing clouds,
Hovering over,
The wind is rising.
Brown shrivelled leaves,
Begin to fall.
Trees are bare,
Stripped of cover.
Tree branches are shaking,
The sky is darker,
Air is colder.
Night has conquered,
Frozen flakes are drifting down,
Early morning dew turns to frost.

Tom McCallum (12)
Dulwich College

AUTUMN POEM

An autumn day is a windy day
Filled with an array of multicoloured leaves
Floating in an azure sky
As though being carried by an invisible hand.

Then suddenly the sky turns gloomy and dark
And the thunderous patter of the rain
Falls onto unsuspecting window sills.

Then how the cool summer breeze
Comes, it goes and the
Autumn coldness freezes over taking its place.

As I walk the leaf swallows ground
They crumble and then another layer of
Dead leaves fall to the victim of
Thousands of feet.

Derrick Odame-Obiri (11)
Dulwich College

MY SILVER BIRCH TREE

As it glistens in the sunlight,
We know the winter's coming,
The green leaves turning orange and gold,
The ochre leaves crackle and crunch under your feet.

The crows and pigeons sitting on the highest branches,
Its wood so smooth,
The long silvery white trunk reaching out,
The thin white branches hanging over,
They are like animals claws, talking to you in the autumn air.

The silver branches sway in the wind,
The silver birch towers over the garden,
Its twigs fall through the air,
As the leaves shrivel up.

The small green creatures living on the twigs and leaves
The maroon seed pods bursting through the small twigs
We know that winter has arrived.

Liam Scannell (12)
Dulwich College

SPELL

Thrice the vixen howled in pain
Thrice the black mare shook her mane
The harpy cries, ''Tis time - it's plan,'

Roundabout the cauldron go
Hazel twigs and yew below
Slimy slug and fresh frogspawn
Heart of babe not 10 days born
Into the pot they all must go
Thrice stirred the way the moon doth go.

Double, double toil and trouble
Fire burn and cauldron bubble.

Underneath the embers rake
In the cauldron boil and bake
Wart of chin and hair of nose
Eagle claw and nail of toe
Rabbit fur and vampire fang
Rancid pigeon left to hang
See the cauldron hiss and bubble
Stir the brew and watch it double.

Skin of snake and beetle shell
Spiky horn from Devil's hell
The ghostly dead arise and yell
To tie the curse into the spell
Deadly nightshade wrapped with web
Spun by spiders as tide doth ebb
End the life that hangs by thread.

Double, double toil and trouble
Fire burn and cauldron bubble.

Cool it down with shards of ice
Then test the charm on three blind mice.

Eliot Williams (11)
Dulwich College

THE BIG TREE

As I wake up,
I draw back the
Curtains and
See the snow on
The lush grass.
I see you
Swaying in the wind.

You can survive anything,
You are invincible,
Your leaves are a magnificent
Green in summer and
A vivid orange in autumn.
When you are bare,
I do not care.

The big tree you are,
You will always
Be that to me.
Even when your end has come,
I will remember you
With all my heart,
Because if I lose you tree,
It will be like losing me.

Jack Goulston (11)
Dulwich College

MAGIC SPELL

All
Hubble, bubble, toil, and trouble,
Fire burn and cauldron bubble.

Witch 1
Mix the lead from a slimy rock
With a foot from a smelly sock,
Scrape the fungus from a hairy armpit,
Blend it gently with a dozen nits
Put in the cat from a witch's hat,
Add on the rat from under the mat.

All
Hubble, bubble, toil and trouble,
Fire burn and cauldron bubble.

Witch 2
Delicious guts from a pig's insides
Boiling and stewing in a saucepan big and wide
The rotting paper in the yard,
All mixed up with greasy lard.
The mouse's tail wrapped in a bat's skin,
Beaten flat with my magic rolling pin!

All
Hubble, bubble, toil and trouble,
Fire burn and cauldron bubble.

Witch 3
The specks from a mangy wolf's coat,
Blood-red liver from a female goat.
All the manure from the farmer's cart,
Reach right in and grab a corpse's heart.
The staring eye of a fat bullfrog
Stirred around with the bladder of a dog.

All
Hubble, bubble, toil and trouble,
Fire burn and cauldron bubble.
Mix it all up and serve with a roll,
Have it on a plate or in a bowl!

Alexander Saunders (11)
Dulwich College

APPLES AND PEARS

In the wilderness of my garden,
You must come and see,
Where the air is clear and lazy,
Stand my apple and pear trees.

They stand up tall and never slouch,
Like soldiers being recruited,
While I am lying on the couch,
They make me look stupid.

I cannot wait until the time,
The apples shed the tree,
Then Mum will bake an apple pie,
Especially for me.

Outside we watch the ripening pears,
With greedy anticipating stares,
I hope my dad will make a tart,
I have a yearning from the heart.

Now the burdened branches have shed their treasure
And we have enjoyed the tasteful pleasure,
The half-naked branches of the trees,
Sway restlessly in the autumn breeze.

Adam Griffiths (11)
Dulwich College

THE SILVER BIRCH TREE

I could have been in deepest Siberia,
As a white blanket appeared, lying on my garden.
It covered everything.

But one tree was still visible,
Its branches were like snakes staying still.
The bark was like the nib of a fountain pen.

It was a giant compared with everything else in sight.
A proud robin was making itself comfortable.
It was singing a song that sounded as sweet as sugar.

A light then came into my eyes and dazzled my vision,
The tree stood almighty, proud and confident,
The sun had arrived and stated its place.

I felt small, worthless and stupid,
The tree and the sun were as old as time
And time brings wisdom.

Yari Voropayev (11)
Dulwich College

TREE IN MY GARDEN

Tree in my garden,
Bare and old,
Tree in my garden,
Goes warm to cold.

Tree in my garden,
You were proud and tall,
Tree in my garden,
You've taken a fall.

Tree in my garden,
Now you're not here,
Tree in my garden,
I look through my tears.

Michael Oliver (11)
Dulwich College

THE DOOR AND WHAT IS BEHIND IT

The door opens,
behind it lie all the answers,
mocking those that are not behind the door,
waiting to get in,
waiting to be answered.

Behind the door,
all problems are solved,
everything dissolves,
there is only the other side,
you cannot return.

The door keeps,
all who go through it,
they cannot escape,
they are trapped,
behind the door.

The door is the end,
the destination of all roads,
you cannot avoid it,
the door is there,
and it waits,
and waits,
and waits,
for us!

Christopher McKeon (11)
Dulwich College

THE WITCHES' SPELL
(Inspired by The Witches' Spell from Macbeth)

Witch 1
Twice the battered wolf hath cried,

Witch 2
Thrice the scorched bat hath sighed,

Witch 3
Now red-eyed rat hath died, 'tis time, 'tis time.

Witch 1
Inside the cauldron pot, mice blood goes; very hot.
Talon of hawk, eye of toad,
Decaying hand, slugs and mould.
Toe nails sliced, newt liver thrice,
Human spine, snail shell slime.

All
Hubble, bubble toil and trouble,
Fire burn and cauldron bubble.

Witch 2
Blood and brain
From wolf untamed,
Hoof of pig
And rotting fig.

Witch 3
Scale of snake
Dweller of lake,
Tooth of shark
Skin of aardvark.

All
Hubble, bubble toil and trouble,
Fire burn and cauldron bubble.

Witch 1
Seal it with a drip of horse blood,
Now the charm has been sung. It is
Done.

Wofai Eyong (12)
Dulwich College

DOWN TO THE GROUND

Tree, tree follow me,
Before you get cut down to the ground.
Before you get disrespected by a hound,
Down to the ground.
You will be used for a wardrobe in IKEA,
Down to the ground.
You will become my paper, my closet,
Down to the ground.
Hurry pick up your legs and run.
Down to the ground,
The cutters have come.
Down to the ground.
Quickly.
Down!
Down!
Down to the ground.

Tobi Akingbolagun (12)
Dulwich College

LIFE AS A TREE

It is nice being a tree,
I am an enormous tree that stretches into the sky,
Full of leaves on lots of thick branches.

I was born during a warm spring with a chilling wind,
I was born in a large crowded park in 1970,
Now I am 32 years old with no leaves,
Autumn is a miserable time,
I look like a death tall stick without any leaves.

I can hear the people stepping on my fallen leaves,
Children are playing and having fun,
While I am standing frozen and miserable.

Winter is even worse and I am even more miserable,
Lots of kids are throwing snowballs at each other
And being wildly overjoyed, waiting to get their Christmas
Presents in their warm houses next to their Christmas trees.

After a while spring will come with new seeds of trees
And the seasonal cycle will continue,
While I will become older and older.

Summer is the best!
The sun is shining and I am full of green leaves,
Summer is full of beautiful flowers and singing birds!
Everyone is on holiday enjoying themselves
And I am too on holiday, relaxing in the warmth of summer,
Summer is the most marvellous season out of them all!

George Draganov (11)
Dulwich College

THE CAULDRON

Witch 1:   Thrice the raven hath flown near,

Witch 2:   Twice the owl's hoot is clear

Witch 3:   And one wailing of a deer,

All: It all means, Macbeth is here

Witch 1:   Stoat's tongue, weasel's dung,
Leg of rhino that weighs one ton,
Bearded camel's hard hump,
Powdered eye of catfish lump,
Beetle's shell in pond water,
Two little lambs straight from the slaughter.

Chorus: Nettle, mettle, watch the petal,
To and fro and the broth will settle.

Witch 2:   Three kilos of whale blood,
Skin of hippo and its mud,
Spleen of turkey, eardrum of chick,
Heart of duck and vodka kick,
Cat's pancreas, dog's bone,
Toenail of a man with a thousand pound loan.

Chorus: Nettle, mettle, watch the petal,
To and fro and the broth will settle.

Witch 3:   Earwax of sow, nostril of cow
A pelican's beak that tastes sour,
Forty-five pairs of bluebottle wings,
Twenty-seven deadly honeybee stings,
Trunk of elephant, eight foot six,
Liver of bat - it's all in the mix.

Thomas Eadon (11)
Dulwich College

THE APPLE TREE

I wander in my garden,
To find an apple tree
I check for fruit but nothing is there.

Not 1, not 2, but 3 months have passed
And yet nothing has come.
I find the tree is alive but
Very much lifeless.

A year has passed and the fruit has grown,
I taste the grapes
Always sweet but never sour,
I have some blackberries,
Never a bad thing.

Now I finally come to the apple tree,
Yet again it has disappointed me,
I say to myself,
Should I really keep this stupid tree?
But then again it might surprise me.
As usual I let it be,
Hoping for a change of luck.

The following day I check my tree,
To my amazement an apple is growing,
Could it be because I spared the tree?

I go to sleep thinking about the apple
And what it tastes like
Because it is the first and may be the last.

I wake up and run outside,
To see an apple half-eaten by a bird.

But I was right about one thing, it was the last.
Now instead of feeding the birds in the park,
I scare them just to get my revenge.

Steven Edmonds (12)
Dulwich College

THE HOLLY TREE

The holly tree in autumn;
Dripping razor barbs from its branches,
Hoping a child will come and step on them.
Jagged knives viciously flying through the air
Hoping they will cut somebody.

The holly tree at Christmas;
Beautiful white slush among fiery poisonous berries.
They hang, desperately trying to escape from birds,
Their only source of destruction.

The holly tree in spring;
Happiness burns in it, as it grows back its prized weapons.
Baby spines are deadly too.
Its evil mind plotting its next assault
Dreaming about spilt blood.

The holly tree in summer:
The roots are squirming with excitement.
The bark's evil spikes shaking.
The berries explode.
Whack! It has been done.

William Bennett (11)
Dulwich College

THE SPELL

Witch 1
Thrice the sacred frog hath barked

Witch 2
Thrice the sacred dog hath mewed

Witch 3
Harpier cries 'Is time, is time,'

Witch 1
All around the cauldron go
In the frozen vomit throw
Fungi that under large tomb stone
Daylight seen has almost none
Inside it is frozen snot
All this goes in the charmed pot

All
Double, double toil and trouble
Fire burn and cauldron bubble

Witch 2
Tail of Greenwich rat
In the cauldron you go *splat!*
Eye of squid and toe of spider
Wool of ewe and tongue of tiger

Witch 3
Scale of snake, tooth of bat
Witches' pig covered in fat
Of the cauldron that is so black
The witches surround it back to back
Horn of half-starved kid
This delivered by a hag
Wrapped up in a magic bag

All
Double, double toil and trouble
Fire burn and cauldron bubble

Witch 2
Seal it with the kiss of death
The curse is helpful to Macbeth.

Thomas Yee (11)
Dulwich College

PINE TREE

I look at a tree,
A spiky pine tree,
Its spindly body protected
By an armour plate of shortened
Lances. The pine sways in
The wind like a great
Mace swinging after
Taking down its
First victim.
Its pine cones
Fall gracefully
Like petals
From a rose;
They land
In the soft
Cushion of
Dewy grass
And roll away
Ready to grow
Into a mighty
Pine tree.

George Lindsell (11)
Dulwich College

WHERE WAS I?

Where was I when the sun left?
Did she say goodbye?
Where was I when it began to get dark?
Was I sleeping?
Where was I when girls stopped wearing summer dresses?
Did they tell me?

When did the conkers start falling?
Did they warn me?
Where was I when the birds stopped tweeting?
Did they say bye?

Where was I when the children started playing with leaves?
Did they remind me?
Where was I when the leaves started changing colour?
Was I sleeping?
Where was I?

Anu Ogunbiyi (11)
Dulwich College

AUTUMN POEM

As you step outside in the morning
The hairs on the back of your neck stand up.
The air is cool and makes your lungs fill with fresh air,
Which adds to the coldness.

The large amount of leaves are like a crunchy carpet
That's very colourful.
The leaves float down like a small boat on a calm sea.

It always seems to be raining and the wind always howling
But the sun creeps in occasionally
Making a kaleidoscope of colour.

Josh Smith (11)
Dulwich College

I WISH I WERE YOU!

Your long blonde hair is almost gold,
But mine is brown and smells like mould,
Your short, sweet laugh attracts the boys,
But mine just makes a load of noise!

Your nails are long with white French tips,
But mine are short and I bite them to bits,
Your skin is clear and you haven't a spot,
But mine is greasy and I hate it a lot!

Your legs are thin, you're very tall,
But mine are fat and I hate being small,
Your dad is rich and he's handsome too,
But mine is dumb and hasn't a clue.

I wish I were you!

Danielle Bowbrick-Moran (12)
Eltham Hill Technology College For Girls

LIFE

People should be able to walk down the street without fear of attack,
People should not be held prisoner,
People should not be judged by their colour, faith or background,
Children should go to school and come back with a smile not a bruise,
People everywhere should have the food, shelter and drink they need,
This country should not have to have prisons,
Children should not wake up with the fear of war,
I know that these things will never come true,
But that is my ideal life.

Stephanie Crouch (12)
Eltham Hill Technology College For Girls

AND I FORGAVE...

Did you recognise my face,
When I walked up to you today?
Was it a flicker of remembrance in your eye,
Of the ways you made me pay?

You'd call me names and pick on me,
Pinch me and pull my hair,
Bang my head against the wall,
You giggle, you sneer, you stare.

I'd hide the bruises from my mum
And cry myself to sleep at night,
I thought it was somehow my fault,
I felt too weak to fight.

I'd never done anything to hurt you,
Not like you did to me,
I was just a popular girl
And you were green with jealousy.

One day Mum found me weeping
And I told her all about you,
She burst into tears and hugged me hard,
She told me I needed to start a new.

And here I am, facing you,
Just like I'm an equal,
Telling you I'm not afraid,
Telling you how I feel.

I'm not going to bully you,
Or get the others to beat you up,
Because you're the one with the problems
And I just want to help.

We're best friends now, together forever,
You changed your ways . . . and I forgave . . .

Charlotte Hey (12)
Eltham Hill Technology College For Girls

THE WORLD IS LIKE AN APPLE

The world is like an apple
Big, harmless and green!
It fills me up with sweetness
And makes me smile with glee!

It's packed with juicy gossip
And lovely people too
It's crunchy, yummy and tender
And love there is stuck like glue!

How good it is to have a world
Filled with things to do
You take one bite, get full of excite
Mmmmm . . . it's tasty too!

Why would I choose an apple
To represent our world?
Because it's teeming with love and sweetness
And feels like it's made out of gold.

So our world is like an apple
And why would I choose that?
Cos when crammed with goodness and love
It turns out really fat!

Rachel Walters (12)
Eltham Hill Technology College For Girls

MY WAY OF LIFE - BEING HOMELESS

On the streets wandering alone,
Feeling helpless, lost and unknown,
Begging for money from passers-by,
Living a dream, living a lie.
Going for days without food or sleep,
Finding most of the time all I do is weep,
I can't go back to what I left,
People murdered, wondering if I'd be next.
Some people and this is true,
Act like they know but they don't have a clue.
It feels like no one's your friend,
When you're on the streets,
So you immediately trust anyone you meet,
Beggars can't be choosers, when you're poor like me,
So I rely on charity and cups of free tea,
Some of the people on the streets give you hope,
They help you out, show you the ropes,
It can be rough, but it's the only way,
Without the streets, I wouldn't be who I am today,
The streets teach me to look after myself
And not look at life as luxuries and wealth.

Jade Solomon (13)
Eltham Hill Technology College For Girls

CHRISTMAS

Christmas night,
Warm fire, shining bright.

White snow,
Candles in the twilight glow.

Choirs singing,
Sleigh bells are ringing.

Children waiting
For Santa by the grating.

Excited faces waiting,
For presents to arrive.

Natalie Howard (12)
Eltham Hill Technology College For Girls

THE WORLD

The world is full of people,
The world is full of countries,
The world is full of cultures,
This world is a big world!

The world is full of joy,
The world is full of laughter,
The world is full of happiness,
The world should stay this way.

The world is full of thirst,
The world is full of poverty,
The world is full of wars,
What are we going to do?

The world is full of wonders,
The world is full of places,
The world is full of nationalities,
We're all part of this world!

Let's build the joy,
Let's build the laughter,
Let's build the happiness,
For the rest of this world!

Poonam Fatania (13)
Eltham Hill Technology College For Girls

FOR MY GREAT GRANDMOTHER - I WASN'T READY TO LET YOU GO

I wasn't ready to let you go
You left us with no warning,
Beneath your suffering,
You smiled, warm and bright.

I wasn't ready to let you go,
I miss you so much,
You're still alive in our hearts,
The one and only Maisie Elaine Lewis,
Your passing away brought indescribable pain.

I wasn't ready to let you go,
The hurting stung so bad,
Nan, we weren't ready to let you go,
We miss your warm, happy, loving glow,
Irreplaceable you are,
You're my guiding star.

I wasn't ready to let you go,
I love you more than words can say,
There's not a day gone when I haven't thought of you,
Just one more hug, one more kiss,
I'll be content, in absolute bliss,
Rest in peace,
We love you Nan.

I wasn't ready to let you go,
Though every time the sun shines, the rain falls,
I know you're there for us,
I'll never ever forget you Nan,
Your great granddaughter Lauren Elaine.

Lauren Colfer (12)
Eltham Hill Technology College For Girls

I WISH I WAS . . .

I wish I was a bird,
So I could soar above the trees,
My life would be much better,
Because I would fly anywhere I required.
If I was a bird.

I wish I was a character,
From my favourite book,
Fighting the forces of evil,
I would be fantastic,
The great, the mighty,
If I was the character from my favourite book.

I wish I was a colour,
Blue, I think is best,
Bright, bold and beautiful,
I would be the sky, the sea and ink,
All in the same day,
If I was the colour blue.

I wish I was the pen,
That wrote the smartest things,
I may not get much gratitude,
But I would know I wrote down good,
If I was that pen.

I wish I was the hands,
The God, who formed all,
I would make the Earth a better place,
Life would be simple, the world unreal,
If I were he who created the world.

Rebecca Chambers (12)
Eltham Hill Technology College For Girls

WHY CAN'T EVERYBODY FLY?

I love to fly high, high, high,
I love to be in the sky,
All the clouds and all the birds are beautiful,
The aeroplanes turning and just carrying passengers,
Why can't everybody fly?

It isn't hard you just spread your wings and take-off,
If everybody flew, you wouldn't need vehicles
And the world would be full of clouds,
So why can't everybody fly?

Is everybody afraid they'll fall?
Are they scared of landing?
Where will the houses go, in the air?
Nobody can explain, they just say,
Why can't everybody fly?

Will you need a test?
Will you have to study?
Is it a waste of time?
Will you care or be reckless?
Nobody can answer the questions, they just say,
Why can't everybody fly?

Just tell me would you like to fly?
Would you want to spread your arms and fly?
Would you love to fly and not walk?
Nobody knows, they just say,
Why can't everybody fly?

Ruth Oyewole (11)
Eltham Hill Technology College For Girls

THE WRONG KIND OF LOVER

Why are you like this
Especially with me?
I hate being trapped
I like to be free.

My emotions locked up,
I'm alone, in hiding,
There's no one to talk to,
No one to confide in.

I need to get out,
I'm going insane,
You're driving me crazy,
You put me through pain.

You say that you love me,
But it seems you don't care,
You make me feel guilty,
I don't think it's fair.

I'm telling you it's over,
I'm putting my foot down,
Get out of my life,
Just get out of town.

No more you,
Now it's just me,
I'm no longer trapped,
I am now free . . .

Katherine Johnson (12)
Eltham Hill Technology College For Girls

THE IRON MAN

Coming out of the sea,
Bursting with rage,
Being stared at,
As if in a cage.

Being so different,
I thought it not a bad thing,
But no one sees beyond this iron body,
The telephone never rings.

Made out of iron,
Stiff as can be,
Never blended in,
I'm lonely, yes lonely,
Won't you be my company?

The nights are cold,
Darker than normal,
The mornings are boring,
Painfully formal.

Being destroyed from the iron heart,
Eventually hurting every part,
Fading away,
Into thin air,
Fading away,
But no one seems to care.

Now finding a friend,
A boy of a young age,
I am now an individual,
No longer in a cage.

Smiling for the first time,
My life finally has sunshine.

Karen Whyte (12)
Eltham Hill Technology College For Girls

THE WORLD

When it snows
And I look out of the window,
It looks like a white picture,
Painted on top of a hill.

The sea is a blue bed,
A blue bed for sharks, fish and whales,
It is a very big, blue bed,
Even bigger than a king-sized bed.

The sun is a beach ball,
Kicked up to the sky,
Up to the beautiful sky,
The sky is like a velvet cloth,
Laid upon over us,
High above us.

The moon is different than everything,
It shines and shows us its sparkles,
It never comes on its own,
It always brings the stars with him,
The stars are like little diamonds,
Which shine on the black desert.

The flowers are a part of our lives,
Sometimes they mean a lot to us,
Just like us they have feelings,
People break their feelings by picking them,
Throwing them and stepping on them,
They want to be left alone,
Alone, just like we would want to be left alone.

When I sit thinking about all these incredible things,
I think I am having a dream.

Rabia Ali (13)
Eltham Hill Technology College For Girls

I . . .

I wonder
I wonder why I am 'me'.
I mean I know about the scientific part
But there must be more
More that hasn't got to do with science
There just has to be!

I wish
I wish I could fly
I wish I could see the whole world beneath me
I watch the news and see people suffering. That's all I see!
I wish I could see the good stuff. The stuff that is never on the news.
I wish the suffering, poverty and hunger could stop and everyone
Will be able to live in peace and harmony.
But then again, 'I wish!'

I believe
I believe I will travel - travel and see the world
Visit every country in every continent
Visit the capital cities of every country
I believe that one day I would be able to see life
Through another kid's eyes
I believe I would do this! But when?

I am
I am only a fourteen-year-old girl.
You might say I have a whole life ahead of me
I should be grateful for everything I have
I know that some people would do anything
To have everything I hate
But what can I do?
I am only 'me'!

Ozge Gunes (14)
Eltham Hill Technology College For Girls

IF EVERYBODY . . .

'Mind the gap.' 'Mind the gap.'
Monday morning at the train station,
People pushing,
Hustling and bustling,
Late for work,
Rushing.

Beep, beep,
Rush hour on the road,
Traffic jams,
Fumes releasing,
People shouting,
Crammed together,
Stop!

If everybody did stop rushing and started relaxing
The world would be a much better place.
If everybody sat still and listened - to the silence,
To the birds singing, to everything they usually miss,
They would find joy and happiness.
If everybody looked around and watched - the children playing,
The creatures around us, the things they usually miss,
They would find peace.
If everybody took notice of every little joy,
The small things that make big differences,
Then maybe we would be more caring,
Always happy, calm and peaceful.
There are so many beautiful things in the world
That people take for granted - lush green plants,
Flowing water, sunshine, even the air we breathe,
But of course, we don't have time to notice these things.

Megan Thompson (13)
Eltham Hill Technology College For Girls

LIFE CYCLE

One year old, crying all the time, my mum is reading me my
favourite nursery rhyme.
Two years old, not roaming free, my mum won't let go of me!
Three years old, moaning all day, I wish my parents would
just go away!
Four years old, starting nursery today, all I want to do is play,
play and play!
Five years old, finding school boring, my bum hurts because
of this hard school flooring.
Six years old, drawing on all of the walls, all my friends are funny
fools.
Seven years old reading my birthday card, it is really, really hard.
Eight years old, my friends really hate school, I am playing a
game of football.
Nine years old, my friends think teachers are sad, I don't and
I am really glad.
Ten years old, playing out with friends, they are driving me
round the bend.
Eleven years old, watching the rising sun, it is not really fun!
Twelve years, in my mouth is my pen, thinking this cycle will happen
over and over again.

Bobbie-Jade Clarkson (12)
Eltham Hill Technology College For Girls

ME

One year old, shouting all day wanting to play.
Two years old, moaning all night getting a fright.
Three years old, I scream for an ice cream.
Four years old, what I want to do all day is play, play, play.
Five years old, went to a party and then felt a little bit arty.
Six years old, learning to read then got hungry and wanted a feed.
Seven years old, I've got a cold and now I'm getting old.

Eight years old, now I'm in school, I have a friend that's a fool.
Nine years old, I've got a cold now, I'm getting big and bold.
Ten years old, growing tall and playing football.
Eleven years old, got homework to do,
All this homework is making me blue.
Twelve years old, all the teachers are a bore and
Outside it's starting to pour.

Gemma Louise Williams (12)
Eltham Hill Technology College For Girls

GREY OUTLOOK ON THE WORLD

All is grey,
Gunfire heard in the distance,
All is grey,
Fighting, shouting and hurting,
All is grey,
Mothers and babies screaming and crying,
All is grey,
Hatred and conflict in the world around us.
All is grey,
People lying dead before us,
Suddenly a bright light shines in the distance and
Everything stops,
Gun fire stops,
Shouting, fighting, people stop,
Mothers and babies' screams stop,
Hatred and conflict stops,
People dying stops,
Everyone lives in peace and harmony,
All is grey in the world today but we hope
The future's bright.

Emma Neill-Elliott (13)
Eltham Hill Technology College For Girls

ALONE

Lost and alone, no place to call home,
Walking the street at night.
Can't see my hand in front of my face,
Except from the old burnt down place,
By the second street light.
Moon in the sky, head in the clouds,
This is all left here for me.
No family or friends, this is my reality,
Lost, never seen this place before.
Alone, never felt any different before.

Lost and alone no place to call home,
I can feel the dark.
I have learnt to live alone, I must feel it all.
Lost in my own world I can believe it's not true.
That I have a place that I belong to.

Natalie Boom (12)
Eltham Hill Technology College For Girls

WE ARE ALL THE SAME ON THE INSIDE

People come in many shapes,
But we are all the same on the inside.

People come in many colours,
But we are all the same on the inside.

People come in many sizes,
But we are all the same on the inside.

People come in many religions,
But we are all the same on the inside.

No matter what we look like, how we act
Or what we believe in,
We are all the same on the inside.

And no one can change that.

Charlotte Price (13)
Eltham Hill Technology College For Girls

CRIME

When bad boys hang around in the street
What are they waiting for?
When you hear of innocent children being hurt
Why did the people do it?
When terrorists take over planes,
Was there any need to hurt innocent people?
If you think about these people they were wrong,
They took harmless people's life into their crime filled hands,
They made the decisions so they should face the consequences,
They should be looked up in prisons,
But they'll get out again,
They should be executed,
But other people will follow in their paths,
Crime will go on forever,
All we can do is try and be safe,
Because crime is our enemy and it hurts.

Fastima Conteh (13)
Eltham Hill Technology College For Girls

THE BULLY

The bully, she came up to me today,
Said spiteful things
And kicked me hard.

The bully, she came up to me today,
I got worried,
There was no knowing what she would do,
It might be a flick, a word or a kick.

The bully, she came up to me today,
But I decided to be strong,
I stood up for myself
And told her where to go.

The bully, she came up to me today,
She was kind,
She was good
Because now she's my friend . . .

Becky Hogwood (12)
Eltham Hill Technology College For Girls

HOMELESS

He wears a coat full of holes,
Ragged, torn and old,
People think he's second rate,
'You're selfish, uncaring and cold!'

He has nothing but a pair of socks,
A scarf and an old rag,
But still he finds he has to sleep
On a bin liner bag.

And here he sits all day long,
Chanting for someone to give,
But no one comes and rescues him,
What a sad life to live.

Catherine Kay (12)
Eltham Hill Technology College For Girls

FREEDOM

Freedom is what makes life worth living,
Destiny is what gives us hope.
Individuality is what gives us friendship,
Romance is what gives us love.

Hate is what gives us danger in our lives,
Thought is what gives us peace,
Money is what gives us enemies,
Shelter is what gives us home.

Life without meaning is a life not yet born,
Death is just a new beginning,
Time is what gives us a bright future,
Even if we don't have a good past.

Family is what gives us importance,
Offspring is what makes us proud,
Justice is what gives us security,
Nature is what gives earth colour.

Freedom is what makes life worth living,
Destiny is what gives us hope,
Individually is what gives us friendship,
Romance is what gives us love.

Emma Hunt (12)
Eltham Hill Technology College For Girls

I IMAGINED . . .

I imagined a world where all were equal,
Where no one was scared to show their face,
I dreamt of a world where all were equal,
No matter their creed, colour or race.

I imagined a world where there was no war
And only peace reigned supreme,
I dreamt of a world where there was no war
And things like violence and fights were a dream.

I imagined a world where the air was clean,
Where thick black fog couldn't be,
I dreamt of a world where the air was clean,
From the highest skies to the sea.

I imagined a world where love was shown,
Where it wasn't just a word thrown about,
I dream of a world where love was shown,
Erasing all downfalls and doubt.

They say that the world we live in is modern,
That we should be proud of it and should stand tall,
But if you weigh the costs against the benefits,
We haven't gained anything at all.

Melody Hodge (13)
Eltham Hill Technology College For Girls

BEST FRIENDS

Best friends are hard to find,
They should be truthful, caring and kind,
Once you have found them, treat them right,
Because friends are an important thing in life.
Always be there when a friend is down,

Never let them show a frown,
You can always trust a real friend,
Be true to them and your friendship will never end.
You need a friend to be there no matter what
And if they're not, they should be forgot.

Chloe Murphy (12)
Eltham Hill Technology College For Girls

A POEM ABOUT OUR WORLD

We're out there on the stars,
A patch of different colours all mixed together,
We form a union, but we don't become one,
We fight with other countries and destroy their homes,
Are we the ones who start the wars or do you start
Them with a careless threat?
The Far East, America and Britain - do we start the wars?
We kill thousands and make people homeless, then the fighting ends.
We don't say sorry or goodbye, we just leave.
When we're in trouble, we beg to other countries
Asking them for help.
'Why should we help you?' they say.
If they don't help us, do we say, 'Now you'll pay?'
If we were meant to be a union, why do we fight,
Kill and destroy other's lives?
Here's a poem within a poem -
Peace is what we want for a nation worldwide,
In some places, it's difficult to find,
Instead of peace we have death, fighting and war,
Nowhere is safe,
There's nowhere to hide,
In our world we fight, we kill and we die.

Jessica Smith (13)
Eltham Hill Technology College For Girls

THE WORLD

The world is a magical place,
Full of life, love and grace.
There are so many people from all different backgrounds,
So much excitement which makes their hearts proud,
Sometimes there's a fear of war which is a worry,
But deep down the fighters are feeling sorry,
The world has lots of places to go,
It's as if it's a never-ending show.
Everyone has good times in the world through the years,
Even though there may be times when they shed tears,
Lots of feelings are spread and shared,
Some are happy, mad and also scared.
The world can have its ups and downs,
But everyone can turn around their frowns.
This large planet has many creatures,
Each with different features,
Many animals roam this land,
From the ocean bed, to the desert sand,
The starry sky comes at night
And the sun comes to wake with its powerful light,
The day is woken by the beautiful bird song,
So we are ready for a day that's 24 hours long,
The world is beautiful I hope you agree,
So let's look after it, that means you and me!

Tamara Jamieson (12)
Eltham Hill Technology College For Girls

VOICES

The soft flow of the stream,
Cascading over the smooth rocks,
Birds singing in the treetops,
Calling to each other in the summer breeze.
The huge willows and oaks,
Hunching over to create some shade,
The tropical fish in the streams,
Leaping as if in a frenzied dance
And the voices,
As pure as gold,
As quiet as a whisper,
Yet as clear as a crystal,
The words call to you,
Tugging at your heart,
Bringing peace and calm,
Yet also company and warmth,
You reach out as if to touch them,
But you cannot touch (that which you hear)
So you laugh,
So do the voices.
Together for two make a delicate harmony,
Surrounding both of you in an aura of tranquillity,
Then you wake,
Remembering the voices, but not all the words,
Last one; Dream!

Hana Dodi (13)
Eltham Hill Technology College For Girls

A HAPPY HEART

When the sun comes up,
Why not go for a joy
Instead of lying in bed and
Becoming a big slob.

Your heart will be happy
If you eat fruit and veg,
Put down that cake
And have an apple instead.

You'll be fit and well if you
Eat treats in proportion,
Avoid colds and coughs
Take vitamin C as a precaution.

Get enough sleep and you'll
Wake up singing,
For good health, long life and
The sense of well being.

Asna Rashid (11)
Eltham Hill Technology College For Girls

FRIENDSHIP

Friendship means you have to share,
You can't just say I do not care.
Friendship means you have to listen,
You can't just ignore and try to glisten.

Friendship means sticking with your friends,
You shouldn't have to make amends.
Friendship isn't about whether you are cute,
You are not supposed to have a dispute.

Friendship is not whether you are intelligent,
You are not supposed to give a bad judgement.
Friendship means all of those things,
So don't break them, they are delicate like rings.

Lauren McNulty (12)
Eltham Hill Technology College For Girls

WEATHER-BEATEN

The weather is a funny thing,
People love it, people hate it,
But haven't people thought about the weather's feelings
And whether it loves or hates you?

I always thought the rainy clouds in the sky,
Were always supposed to be crestfallen and broody
And the sun was contented and blissful,
But what if they swapped personalities?

The sun would hide its sunshine in a curtain of
Swarthy and morbid clouds
And the rainy clouds would adore showering us
With woe and gloom.

Oh, everyone would be depressed and feel cursed,
Upon both rain and sun,
But what if God created a mechanical, push button
Weather chooser?

Everyone would be jubilant and ecstatic,
By God's new creation and live on their lives,
Without the devilish, possessed, manic
Weather.

Yasmin Francis (12)
Eltham Hill Technology College For Girls

LIFE

What is life?
How do we cope?
Explain
And live through it?
When it gets too much,
Where do we escape?
Life is a mystery that we cannot understand!
It is a battle racing to commence,
How do we cope with the downfalls?
How do we cope in times of need?
The loss of a loved one,
Where do we pick up strength to survive?
In times when your goals are not achieved,
Strong perseverance, and will power,
Is the key to unlocking the door to success.
When you fall,
Expect to rise again!
The downfalls of life, is not the end of it!
Everyone has to cope,
With it, and make the most of it.
It all depends on the determination of your heart.
The choices we make,
Change
Our lives,
Our dreams,
Whether good or bad!

Mahar Roy-McCauley (13)
Eltham Hill Technology College For Girls

THE LONELY TIGER

I am a tiger, hungry and lonely
My heart is filled with sorrow.
I never thought I would see the day
When I'd never see the light of tomorrow.

You crushed my soul in too many ways,
I have only lived for 26 days.
Now you'll do what you did with the others
And dispose of me off the Earth.

I am that lonely tiger
Grieving in my cage.
Dying because of you
Not from old age.

I want to roam free
With what's left of my kind.
I do not know what will become of me
That's something I don't want to find.

Please think twice about your abusing
It's only our soft warm fur you are using.
Why don't you make your own
And leave the animals of the world alone?

You haunt my spirit inside of me
When I should be happy, filled with glee.
But no, yet can't you see
There is that soft spot inside of you that can set us free.

For I am the lonely tiger
Grieving in my cage.
Dying because of you
Not from old age.

Rachel Amy Foster (12)
Eltham Hill Technology College For Girls

MY SECRET

I have a boyfriend, he's a lovely lad,
When I'm with him, I'm never sad,
He makes me feel special and I want him to know,
I never want to see him go,
I love him to bits, just wish he could see,
How much he really means to me!
It's definitely love and that's for sure,
Because I've never felt like this before.

When I see him I get a wonderful feeling,
I feel so happy as if I could touch the ceiling.

Amy Raven (13)
Eltham Hill Technology College For Girls

TREE SEASONS

Spring
The tree hums quietly to itself
A lullaby to the buds bursting
With baby leaves its branches
Ride winds in all green glory
Tree begins to sing.

Summer
The tree stretches in the sun
Knows the birds that fly the beasts
From heavy branches and digs roots
Deep into the centre of the spinning earth.

Deva Michael
Henry Compton Secondary School

SCHOOL

In the morning,
You wake up,
You go to the bathroom
And put on the tap.

You get toothpaste
And put it on your brush,
You brush your teeth,
You're not in a rush.

You have your breakfast,
You eat some food,
You put on your uniform,
In a bad mood.

You wait for the bus,
Or the train,
They take so long,
It is a pain.

You get to school
And play a game,
You go to registration,
It's always lame.

First lesson time,
You go to your class,
You line up and wait,
You go in last.

The lesson's dry,
You do not listen,
You're too tired,
To be in a lesson.

There goes the bell,
It is lesson two,
Two lessons until break,
It can't be true.

In periods,
Two and three,
You are so tired,
You can hardly see.

Finally it is,
Time for break,
You have some food,
You really feel awake.

You do the work,
In the next two lessons,
You have more energy,
You're paying more attention.

Now it's lunch,
You play football,
You win the match,
You eat in the food hall.

Last period,
Make it good,
Behave well,
As you should.

The bell goes,
It's the end of school,
You'll have to do homework,
That's not cool.

This might be
The days of school,
Some people go through,
That are not cool.

You have to learn,
When you go to school,
If you don't
You'll be a fool.

Mohammed Kibria (12)
Henry Compton Secondary School

SEASONS

The summer has gone,
T-shirt enough,
Amber waves of grain,
Summer, I love you.

Autumn here you are,
Grab my jumper,
Flying leaves in red and brown,
Autumn, I love you.

Winter on my doorstep,
Scarf and mittens,
A silent blanket of snow,
Winter, I love you.

Spring is on my mind,
Off the coats and the hats
A soft carpet of green grass,
Spring, I love you.

Sascha Wiegand
Henry Compton Secondary School

WHEN THE EYES WATER

Uncontrollably, they water
A steady flow, like that of a river,
For what reason, nobody knows
And nobody tends to care,
How do they allow her to cry?
And why, would it be a crime to ask?
Bearing all within herself
She continues
And accepts circumstances as her fate.
She sees nothing and
Forbids all sound to reach her ears
It seems to her that the watering will never stop,
She tries to stop,
Tries to pat her cheeks dry,
But the river is uncontrollable
And so are her emotions,
Oh why? - Why does she accept all?
Taking an overdose?
Thrusting herself at a vehicle
That speeds at the rate of 90 mph?
No, the eyes are unbearable, and are enough
In a desperate attempt to stop them,
Her fate lets her down once more
And the tragedy sets in for her,
Uncontrollably, they water
A steady flow, like that of a river,
For what reason - nobody knows.

Hina Nàqvi (16)
Plumstead Manor School

THE CONVERSION

The falling swirls of crystal jewels
Fall swiftly from the heavens
They thump the window of the house
The one the locals talk about.

This house they say is full of evil
They tell tales of horror and wickedness
But they do not know who lives there
In fear they would be cursed.

So I went to this evil house
To see what the trouble was about
To end the citizens' lifelong fear
My moment was all so near.

I took a step into its grounds,
To see what could be found,
My eyes were narrowed, listening to any sound
My thoughts were swirling round and round.

I opened the large oak door,
To see what was causing the uproar,
As I went in what I saw . . .
Made me drop my mouth in awe.

A vampire figure stood before me,
It had two fangs and a row of yellow teeth,
I wanted to run but I stood there in fright
And it gave me its fatal bite.

My emotions had flowed out like a flood,
I'd felt an urge for human blood
And as I hid from the candlelight,
I strode outside into the night.

Matthew Kimemia (13)
Riverston School

BULLY, BULLY

Bully, bully,
Why must you hurt me
And beat me black and blue?
What did I do to you?
Is it because you seek attention
Or are you jealous of me?
Maybe because you're scared, alone,
Nervous or isolated?
Maybe you crumble under peer pressure,
I don't want any trouble.

Bully, bully,
All the time I have to watch where I go,
Sneaking, hiding, being careful and watching where I go,
Only because I'm scared of you.

Bully, bully,
You send letters to me but you think I don't know,
I see you through the window putting it on my desk,
With nasty, hurtful words.
Maybe we can be friends some day,
But, only if you stop hurting me!

Christopher Grey (12)
Riverston School

MOON WOLF

Wandering, stalker of the night.
On the hilltop calling to the moon,
The sound of the pack answering back,
'Moon wolf.'

Your sleek dark silhouette strong against the shimmering moonlight.
Your yawn, teeth white, fangs sharp, mouth wide, dark and
Sinister like an undercover tomb.
'Moon wolf.'

Your coat glistens as you dance pass the moonlight.
Something moves, you stand alert.
Your eyes glare in direction of the sound, you sniff the air
'Moon wolf.'

You start to whine as the pack appears,
Home at last, as you all start to howl into the night.
Who is the brave creature of the night?
'Moon wolf.'

Milaner Glean (14)
Riverston School

PIANO

Piano, piano, where are you?
Playing the secrets of the moon,
Piano, piano, I call on you,
Piano, piano, please come soon.

When I hear your sweet melody,
I shall know,
How to play that melody,
Piano, piano, I hear you in the snow.

Bass and treble are your keys,
When you're playing you start with these,
Piano, piano, where art thee?
Piano, piano, please come to me.

Piano, piano, where are you?
Playing the secrets of the moon,
Piano, piano, I call on you,
Piano, piano, please come soon.

Samuel Essien (11)
Riverston School

THE CHEETAH

Running, running, so fast, so light,
A cheetah, comes into sight.

The cheetah,
The faded one,
As powerful as the world,
Well we shall see . . .

Suddenly,
She sees two hunters walk into view,
With shotguns, pistols, knives,
Could this be the end of our magnificent cheetah?

She pricks up her ears at the sound of death,
Bang!
Slice!
Chop!
Goes the knife
And so with this she runs,
Deep into the heart of the rainforest,
Will she survive?

Jack Steadman (13)
Riverston School

THE CONKER

The conker is like a prisoner
Trapped in a shell
With sharp claws and spikes
Ready to attack.

Hanging in a tree
In its prickly case
Until it is ready
To show its face.

When showing its face
It is round and shiny
As if being polished
This prisoner is now free to make
A new tree.

On the ground it will bounce and roll
Free from its shell,
Ready to start a new life,
Where? Who can tell?

Fawaz Akbar Qureshi (11)
Riverston School

NO BREAD!

I wish I'd made a list,
I forgot to get the bread.
If I forget it again,
I'll be dead.

We had blank and butter pudding.

Beans on zip,
Boiled egg with deserters,
No chip butty, just chip.

I wish I'd made a list,
I forgot to get the bread,
My mum got the empty bread bin
And wrapped it round my head.

My mum says if I run away,
She knows I won't be missed,
Not like the bread was . . .
I wish I'd made a list.

Nadia Badawi (12)
Riverston School

THE SUNSET

The sunset is beautiful,
As I look out of my window,
You usually see it over hills and cliffs,
With its golden cloves of light.

Sometimes you wonder what's in the sun,
Especially when it sets,
It has less feeling when it's rising,
Most people seem to think.

You cannot touch the sunlight,
But you can feel its heat,
Then it's time for the sun to set
And the moon begins its shift.

You can think of the sun as a job,
A job that can never be complete,
This is caused by other weather
And how you treat the sun.

This is the sun that you cannot touch,
Doing a non-paid job,
Learn to appreciate the sun,
Like the sun has learnt to appreciate us.

Rhamatalah Ayoade (12)
Riverston School

ANGER

Anger is trigger,
To your temper,
Your rage is a spike,
Spike to your strength,
Your destruction,
Your fear,
Your nightmare!

Your rage is a key,
To your violence,
To shatter,
To cause pain,
To defend,
To offend.

Someone gets hurt,
Nobody cares,
Tears fall out,
Anger goes out of control,
There is no stopping it
It has to be unleashed,
It has to be released,
No matter how one tries,
Anger, never dies.

Ali Moonan (12)
Riverston School

WIND AND LOVE

Love and wind are like a pair,
First comes *love* as happy as
Sun shine, the world cannot
Be a better place at this time.
You think that it will never end.
Then come the sinister one of
The pair, the *wind*. This part of
The pair will rip *love* apart one
Way to another. Twisting *love*
Like a tornado twisting it until
Love turns to hate. But this is not
Always the case, in some cases the
Love pulls through, not enough to
Save the *love* that was felt but to
Change *love* into friendship.

Benjamin Laing (16)
Riverston School

SWEET THOUGHTS

Memories old . . . memories new.
Thoughts of love . . . when I think of you!
Remembering . . . how it used to be.
In my dream . . . it is you I see!
Times gone by . . . some bad . . . some good!
To have them now . . . I wish I could!
Turning back the days and years.
Some filled with love . . . and some filled with tears.
What we have is love so true.
A little of me . . . and a lot of you! As these memories fade away,
It comes to mind the times we shared.
Thinking of my love so true on Valentine's Day I think of you.

Shantel Preece (13)
Riverston School

176

A TIGER'S LOVE

Tiger of the night
So quiet and peaceful,
Sitting with its young sleeping.

Tiger of the day so proud,
Hunting for its young,
Running to catch its prey,
Leaping at great speed,
Tearing at its prey to fill its hunger.

Carrying the food to its young,
Lying closely by its family as they feed.

What difference is there
Between man and beast?

Peter Ashley (13)
Riverston School

PATIENCE

One day,
That time will arrive,
It just might be a while,
So look up, smile
At that thought,
Of that day,
When we'll have the day of a lifetime
And gaze in wonder at that silver dandelion,
That spark,
That light,
That energy,
Which surely,
Lives in both you and me.

Jack Mills Davidson (14)
Riverston School

BULLYING

Bullying.
Why do people bully?
Is it to hurt people's feelings?
Is it to put them down?
There can be verbal or physical bullying
They both hurt.

Bullying.
Why do people bully?
Is it because they got bullied themselves?
Is it because they are under influence?
Cussing,
Fighting,
Threatening,
Blackmailing,
Are all types of bullying.
They all hurt people's feelings,
So why do people bully?

Bethany Gibbs (12)
Riverston School

SPIDER POEM

Fly, fly, come here,
Fly, fly, next to me.
See the world up here,
Why don't you join me?

Bee, bee, o'er there,
Bee, bee, do not scare.
Fly over there and,
Be in my care.

Bugs, bugs, unaware,
Shrugs, shrugs, 'I don't care.'
I am on my web,
It's like a silvery bed.

Out of the blue,
Comes my dinner!
For, I'm a spinner.

Richard Killick (11)
Riverston School

GRAFFITI BOY

He walks the streets with not a care in the world,
The sacks of cans in his left hand,
His work is of such mystery depending on his mood,
The depths of the ocean, the sun, sea and sand.

Why does he expose himself to the wind and the cold?
Into his work he has so much passion,
He is quite a poor fellow with nowhere much to live
And wears his long overcoat in such a worn out fashion.

Why does he stand alone dreaming of his next creation?
Billboards, on the bus, even shop rows,
He only works his magic in the depths of the night,
The abandoned underground in which he moves.

From city to city, across the land, his art is well known,
He hitch-hikes to get about,
He is known as a menace about the village,
That dirty graffiti boy they curse and shout.

Maxine Thompson Reede (14)
Riverston School

THE PRISONER

I look into the eyes of a deprived man,
I see no future, I see no plan,
I see his conviction, I see him disappear,
I see his living conditions and wonder why he's here.

I look into his soul and see nothing but a hole,
If I look too deep, I will fall to sleep,
I look at his heart and see wonderful art,
It sings with colour and smiles without fear.

His time is near, as the atmosphere is swift all around him,
His canvas is clear, his heart is no longer there,
His eyes are white, as he cries with all his might,
His tunnel of light is approaching
And his fingers are eroding.

He has no fear, he has no life left over here,
I now look into the eyes of a free man,
And see . . .

Fatimah Ayoade (14)
Riverston School

WHAT IS LOVE?

What is love?
Is it built on friendship, trust and honesty,
Or is it deceit, lying and jealously?
What is love to you?
Is it all tears and sadness,
Or is it a lifetime full of happiness?

How do you know if you've found your true love?
Does your heart beat every time you see them?
Do you float off to cloud 9,
Or do you count each second when you're apart?
What is love?

Roopa Pancholi (14)
Riverston School

MY JULIET

Reminiscent of a goddess in the clouds you lay
Watching me as I wonder astray
The love and sweetness has been locked in vain
Only a sour taste and bitter pain remains.

An empty void left in an immense hole
Swept away my heart and my soul
Was it to be or not to be?
That your love was meant for me.

That smile, those eyes are all I'll remember,
Your sweetness, that touch that was ever so tender,
Your loving memory is all the beauty that remains,
May you cherish the thought of no more pain.

Like an angel you are, so honest and caring,
I will be more faithful and even less daring,
Knowing that you are what makes my heart excel,
The pain that lives shall never tell.

Reminiscent of a goddess in the clouds you lay,
Watching me as I wonder astray,
The love and sweetness has been locked in vain,
Only a sour taste and bitter pain remains.

William Serwadda (14)
Riverston School

TIME

Time never stands still,
It keeps on moving and always will,
Changes everything does it that,
Funny thing called time.

When you're having fun,
Time always goes fast,
I just want time to stand still,
So that having fun can last.

Time makes you old,
Time turns the weather cold,
Time says, 'It's time for bed.'
It's not really because Mum and Dad has said.

Time is a silent dictator,
Even when we say, 'Oh I'll do it later,'
Time waits for no one,
We wait for time.

Reis Aslan (13)
Riverston School

POWER OF WORDS

Words, how melodically beautiful it is to twist and turn
Them like bodies in the wind.

Standing rigid as headstone
Or as liquid like as the ocean flows.
Melting like summer rays of heat.
Gentle as a baby's murmur.
Pounding like a heartbeat in the writer's mind.

David Arnold (14)
Riverston School

THE SUN

I can see the sun rising,
Above the world,
I can see an open door of
Acceptance in my heart,
I'm proud of myself and my people
This is my world,
It's what I make it,
Not what it makes me.

I can see the sun rising,
The tears are drying,
Our hearts are mending,
Time for change
Happiness and smiling
No more worrying!

I can see the sun rising,
For us and many more to come!
I can see the sun shining for us and
Many more to come.

Victoria Coker (16)
Riverston School

DREAM

Dream for love or dream of a perfect life,
Dream he'll pop the question and the day you become man and wife,
Dream of tomorrow or dream of yesterday,
Dream of time together as time slips away,
Hell dream of a nightmare if you have to,
But don't stop dreaming, no matter what you do,
Dream of perfection as you sleep in your warm bed,
For once you stop dreaming you're found dead.

Danielle Milton (17)
St Francis Xavier Sixth Form College

TONIGHT

They say it can hurt to love someone
That love is an evil that will always cling onto you,
I have been taught to imagine love as a dream
But tonight we will see and witness the meaning of this dream.
I have been told love is blessed and sent by God
That the heart and soul can be someone's eternal bliss.
I know this love can be sent in the form of my wishes,
Tonight we shall see if my prayers have been answered.
A look can be enough to mean something
It can also be an arrow or a dagger
But it can conceal feelings
Tonight we shall see if my glance is returned.
You cannot bring yourself to touch me,
You fear to look me straight in the eyes,
You seem afraid of your heartbeat
Tonight there is an intention on seeing the wounding of my heart.
Love can kill and can be died for,
Just like the flame I hold for you.
Death spreads its cloak to find its next victim,
Tonight, if we survive, we shall see the dawning of a new day . . .

Sergio Coelho (17)
St Francis Xavier Sixth Form College

I CAN'T CHANGE THE CLOCK BACK

I can't change the way things are,
Or make the clock go back,
I can't make life easier,
That's the way life is and that's that.

I've been with family since I was young
And I don't know what to think
I was sent away with my sister
But she's sleeping now, it's late.

Every day is a struggle,
I have nowhere else to go
We are being watched all the time
And I'm feeling alone.

Asha Bacchus (12)
Westwood Language College For Girls

My Family

They're like a big box of ideas if I need help with my homework.
They are a heart giving out all its love.
They're like your best friends but really they're your family.
They're a big bowl of pillows which are soft and cuddly like their hugs.
They're like they are there to represent the five points on a star,
apart from they're not sharp.
They have a piece of Heaven inside them that will never make them
go wrong.
They're like a bag of sweets so they can share them out with everyone.
They are like the sun and they only shine to keep me warm.
They're like a hot cake which has just come out of the oven
so their love is warm.
They are busy bees but they always have time for me.
They're like a big book that has too many hard words in it
but they make it easy for me.
They are a star which sparkles in the midnight sky that leaves
a light beam shining on me.
They're like a dictionary if I need to look something up.
They have the strength of a lion so they use it to protect their children.
They're like an encyclopaedia with so much information stored up.

Zainab Agha (11)
Westwood Language College For Girls

I SAW IT

I saw it
They were running, crying and falling
Houses were blasting, people were dying and collapsing.
I saw it
The country on fire and at war
Helicopters flying in the air
Children were stuck on the street.
They were lost
Couldn't find their way out
I stood there
Screamed for help
There was no one coming
Street full of blood, dust and dead bodies
I saw it
Our house on fire
It was burning
Burning like a bonfire
My parents were gone
Left on my own to cope
It was a matter of life and death
They were coming
Coming like armed soldiers
I ran, but couldn't hide
A gunshot
People screaming to death
I hid myself behind a burnt house
I knew that was it
It wasn't
They were coming
I could hear them
I could hear their footsteps.

Paula Pedanou (14)
Westwood Language College For Girls

THE FOUR STAGES OF MY LIFE

When I was just a baby girl,
My mum could read my mind.

When I was hungry, yes, she knew,
But how did she know about my number 2?

When I was one, I loved to talk,
But most things I said made no sense.
Things like 'lellow' for the colour yellow,
My mum could understand.

When I was two I could walk around,
As confident as could be,
And finally see the world,
Or as it was to me.

When I was three at nursery,
I was what I had planned to be,
Wild, loud, crazy and free,
Until my mum collected me.
I could still be all these things at home,
But there was not so much space,
In this case.

When I was four,
I was getting old.
Starting school,
A change of clothes,
In uniform and a great big yawn.

And from then I am older still,
13 now!
No more happy meals.

Latoya Nelson (13)
Westwood Language College For Girls

THE AGE POEM!

When I was 3,
I hurt my knee,
By falling out of a tree,
My mum came and
Gave me a plaster
So I couldn't walk faster.

When I was 4,
I fell on the floor
And rolled out the door,
Then my pretty little
Dress torn,
My mum shouted,
'You're not crawling anymore!'

When I was 5,
I climbed on a beehive
Then I took a big dive
And my mum hollowed,
'You're only 5!'

Natasha Robertson (12)
Westwood Language College for Girls

THE PARK

The grass is green,
The sky is blue,
On the swing,
Birds start to sing.

On the slide,
Have a ride,
What can I do,
I'm having fun.

Nearly time to go,
At half-past 1,
So I buy an ice cream
And walk to the stream.

I feed the ducks,
A bird sings and a chicken clucks,
It's time to go away
And come another day.

Sajidah Rehman (12)
Westwood Language College for Girls

WHO WILL YOU SEE AT THE GATE?

There goes the bell,
It's half-past three,
Down by the school gate
You will see . . .

Ten mums talking,
Nine babies in their prams, squawking,
Eight dads parking,
Seven dogs barking.

Six toddlers all squabbling,
Five grans on bikes wobbling,
Four childminders smoking,
Three bus drivers choking.

Two teenagers dating,
One lollipop man waiting.

The school is out, it's half-past three
And the first to the gate . . . is me.

Melissa Gordon (12)
Westwood Language College For Girls

DENIED

When I wrote on the wall,
It really wasn't cool,
I denied, I denied, I denied,
Until I cried, I cried, I cried.

My mum asked my brother,
I was like oh bother,
My mum asked my sister,
I tried to resist her,
I denied, I denied, I denied,
Until I cried, I cried, I cried.

I hope she never comes to me,
I'm buzzing like a bee,
She was furious that no one confessed,
While I was really distressed,
My mum asked my dad to look
He looked at it and shock,
I denied, I denied, I denied
Until I cried, I cried, I cried.

My mum and dad turned to me,
Should I say no or yes maybe?
We asked you a question,
It's time for confession.

I denied, I denied, I denied,
Until I cried, I cried, I cried.

Chevon Nicola Jones (12)
Westwood Language College for Girls

CHILDHOOD

Childhood was fun for me,
Childhood was a game.
My father gave me a cat one day,
After meeting my stepmum.
My stepmum was cat mad too,
Though my father was not mad.

Over the years our bond faded,
But till the end we'll always make it.
There were minute fights and arguments
With blades at everyone's throat,
But one would always escape the danger,
Without a scratch, but scared.

Upon the mind these scenes would play,
Keeping me awake through night and day,
Twisted up was I? It seemed,
Scared with one to run.
We stuck together me and Dad,
We can always speak the truth.

Childhood seems a game no more,
It's time to see what's real.
It's time to grow up now,
To gain a better deal.
This way, if I behave mature,
My life behind closed door will be no more.

Dane Sammut (13)
Westwood Language College For Girls

GERMINATION

The air is cold to me,
I can hear a buzzing bee.

I'm swirling around,
I know I'm near the ground,

Waiting . . . waiting.

The time has come, I start to crack,
Lying on my back.
I see the sun,
I want to run.

Waiting . . . waiting.

I'm in a pot,
It's getting hot.

The sun is beaming,
My seed is steaming.

Waiting . . . waiting.

Jade-Olivia Sandy (11)
Westwood Language College For Girls

MY LIL' SIS

She's tiny, annoying, although quite sweet,
She follows me everywhere and eats what I eat.

She sleeps in my room and goes through my phone,
She never ever, leaves me alone.

At times when I look to my left and right,
She's always there in my sight.

Oh please help me,
I'm on my knees.

I hate it when I have to babysit,
Tuck her in with her night light lit.

And finally, when it's the end of the day,
Thank the Lord, I always say.

Siobhan Bailey (13)
Westwood Language College For Girls

PERSONALITY

I like roses, I like pink
I'm a big baby that's why I stink.

I like horses, I like blue
I'm clever and I'm better than you.

I am lazy and I love to be crazy
I am such a pain, I'm so insane.

I'm hardworking and keep talking
I'm so smart, I'm always first to start.

I play with boys and my toys
It's all the same, life's a game.

I get A* and would love to go to Mars
I am very bright and have short sight.

I'm ugly and fair
But I'm proud of my hair.

Amber Karim (13)
Westwood Language College For Girls

THAT FUNNY FEELING

One day I went to the park,
I came back in a really happy mood,
When I came back,
My mum told me she was pregnant,
I was in a dull mood,
I asked my brother, he said yes,
I asked my dad, he didn't know,
I didn't know what to believe,
I went to bed,
Woke up in the night,
Asked my mum if she was pregnant,
She said she would not lie about that,
So like a daft little fool,
I went to bed believing it was true.

Ezarah Gomes (12)
Westwood Language College for Girls

STRANGE NIGHT

One night, strange noises started to come,
They scared me and my scared mum.

I looked out of the window and saw two cats
Chasing some poor, defenceless rats.

I went outside to stop the fight,
But ended up in a fright.

I went back inside
And my mum replied,
'It's time to go to bed.'

And that was the end.

Stephanie Bryan (12)
Westwood Language College for Girls

MY MISTY WINTER

Looking from my frosted window,
People blushing with rough breeze,
Air touching the tip of my cheek,
Even though I'm under my sheet.

Trees were rustling, leaves were dropping,
God was crying tears of rain.

Beyond my eyes mist and sleet was coming,
Down hard and heavy,
Cold fingers and swollen toes
And people with red noses crying out,
'Please help me,'

I bet they wish they were in here with me!

Yasmin Mason (12)
Westwood Language College for Girls

WAITING AND REMEMBERING

I sit here alone waiting for your call,
Wondering will you call at all.
Sitting in my gran's rocking chair,
Thinking this is so unfair.
When I eat wine gums I think of you,
When we were best friends it was so cool.

Do you remember when you were here
And when we first tried beer?
My best friend you're always in my heart
And in my mind we'll never be apart.

Karlishia Rushel Smith (13)
Westwood Language College For Girls

My Choice Is My Family

My choice is my family.
I don't want anything else
Only my family.

At least I can hear someone talking to me
At least I see my family.

Forget everything, everything I had
But don't forget my family.

They are here caring about me.
They are here wiping my tears only.

My brother is here to play with me.
My mother is here to hug me.

My father is here to make me happy
That's all I need.

My choice is my family.

Urmila Pucha (12)
Westwood Language College For Girls

When I Was Six

When I was six
I fell off a swing,
My head was making noises,
Ping! Ping! Ping!

I got back up again
And looked around,
But one second later
I fell back to the ground!

I called for help
But no one could hear me,
Then that was when
I wished I had my own door key!

When my mum came
And picked me up,
She gave me some Coke
In my doggy-patterned cup!

Lauren Walkling (12)
Westwood Language College For Girls

Mum

Mum, Mum,
You're fun,
You're safe
And you're pretty.

Mum, Mum,
You're fun,
You run down hills with us,
You do so much for us.

Mum, Mum,
You do so much for us,
Mum, Mum,
We love you,
Mum, Mum,
You're the best
Mum, Mum.

Shemaiah Bristol (11)
Westwood Language College for Girls

MY OWN BROTHER

It was such a surprise,
I had my own brother,
He must be very soft as soft as a bear,
It felt so exciting,
That I jumped all around.
It was so surprising,
That it made me mad.
When I went to see him,
The guard stopped me,
He said the hospital isn't open
For children every day,
He went back to the cabin
And told me to go away,
But I was so excited
I chose my own way,
I hugged my brother as tight as I could
And cried as long as I could.
The guard came running
And told me to go away,
That didn't matter because
I saw my brother anyway.

Keerti Brar (12)
Westwood Language College for Girls

A YOUNG FELLOW CALLED WRENCH

A greedy young fellow called wrench
Owned a cat, 2 small dogs and a tench.
One day, in a trice,
He cooked them with rice
An called the dish something in French.

Indrina Murugan (11)
Westwood Language College For Girls

MY BROTHER

My brother is a Mars bar,
A sweet and chocolaty one.

My brother shines bright
And as white and fluffy as a cloud.

My brother is a Mercedes Benz car,
With his engine always running.

My brother is as soft as silk
And as red as Jupiter can be.

My brother is like a carpet or a teddy,
Always soft and cuddly.

My brother is as loud as a drum,
But with a tune which is always happy.

My bother is his own planet,
Always bright and sunny.

My brother is sometimes quiet,
But as hot as curry.

However my brother is,
I love him in every way.

Tahban Mokree (12)
Westwood Language College For Girls

SAID THE GENERAL

Said the general of the army,
'I think the war is barmy.'
So he threw away his gun
Now he's having much more fun.

Alaiya Shah (11)
Westwood Language College For Girls

TIME

Time is a virtue,
Or so I've been told.
Time is a curse,
Yet a blessing.
During daytime
There are people and emotions to control.
There is the warmth of the sun,
The blue of the sky.
No one is who they seem,
Time is a curse.
Night is when hell is let loose,
When the angels of the day
Are the demons of the night,
When things and people
Are portrayed in their true form.
Your emotions rule you,
Letting you feel
Fresh, true, pure, real.
The stars give the dark night sky
That slight quality the night sky lacks,
A quality which makes you warm,
Then time is in its kindest form.
Here, time is a blessing,
A virtue.

Diana Monteiro (13)
Westwood Language College For Girls

DO I NEED IT OR JUST WANT IT?

Do I need my make-up?
No
Do I need my friends?
Yes
How about my hair stuff?
No, no I don't
I'll tell you what I need
My mum and my aunt
My brothers and sisters
Oh yeah and my cat and dog
Could I live without TV and PC?
It would be hard but yes
How about my best friend Blessing?
I could never, would never
Or my other friends?
People like Natasha?
No
So I have decided what I need are people
Not material things
I need nothing else
Nothing else is actually very important to me
Just friends, friends and family
And, oh yeah, pets.

Charlotte Pearse (13)
Westwood Language College For Girls

DR NORTON'S ELIXIR

'Tell me again,' the doctor said,
'These symptoms that you feel,
Is it a pain, an ache, or what?
And are you sure it's real?'

'It's real, alright!' the computer said,
'I just can't seem to start!
It keeps me up all the night,
I think I'm going to fall apart!

My brain is all a jumble,
My chips are all askew,
I'm really in a fumble,
I'd like some help from you.

I feel all tingly in my tummy,
There's something in there too!
It makes me feel so very funny,
I think I've got the flu!'

'Oh no you haven't!' the doctor cried,
'It's something else, I'm sure.
It's probably just a virus -
And I think I know the cure.

Dr Norton's elixir should do the trick,
Take it three times every day,
Always tell me when you feel sick,
Now shove off, go away!'

Maisie Pailyn Ireland (12)
Westwood Language College For Girls

DEEP DOWN

Deep down inside me
No one knows how I feel.
Thoughts are spinning round my head,
Wishing someone would come,
To guide me to the right path.
I really wish I could turn back time,
Fix all the bad things.
Deep down, I wish I could be more than
Friends with the one I love.
It feels like I'm losing my mind, going insane.
If only we were together forever as one.
Knowing that it will never come true,
It feels like I'm falling to pieces.
Being friends is not enough for me, deep down
I sometimes feel so empty inside,
Thinking life is not worth living.
Deep down, when I look into your eyes,
I feel my body and soul rise,
My heart aches and beats faster,
Going through so much pain and tears in my eyes,
I really wish I could put things straight.
So here I am alone, sitting on my bed,
With all my love and anger locked up
Deep down inside my heart.
So I guess this is where the story ends,
I have to realise it's forever - goodbye.
He will never be back again,
Even though it will take time
To dry away the tears in my eyes.

Sumayya Choudhury (13)
Westwood Language College For Girls

THE DIRTY BOY OF IRAN ITSELF

Secluded streets,
Dusty, empty homes,
If they speak or run they get the beats.
The dirty boy of Iran itself,
Is left alone to roam.
Whips the timid woman's back,
Husband and child held hostage in a sack,
If there is a chance to go,
Run,
Hide,
They *will* snatch it, without a chance to wonder what to take,
Just leave,
Sea,
River,
Lake,
The dirty boy of Iran itself,
Has gone, adios,
Without a trace,
On the back of a melon boat for the last two hours now,
He has many questions,
Where am I going?
When will I get there?
How?
The dirty boy of Iran itself, has gone to sleep,
The boat is silent, with not a peep,
The engine of the boat is still quiet,
You hear, 'Can we check this boat?' and a riot.
The dirty boy of Iran itself is found.
Still himself,
Dirty, but now floppy-limbed,
Now head with halo golden rimmed,
The clean, pure boy of Iran itself is
Peaceful,
Calm
And sweet.

The journey is over, he's found his peace and God,
The soul has been sent,
He's found his peace and God,
Amen.

Lauren Andrews-Stannard (13)
Westwood Language College For Girls

WAR

There is no choice
A war has broken
I have to go
There is no choice.

My life has changed
Have to get on a boat
I can do without my choice
Do without my toys
But cannot leave . . .

Mum's magic hug
Nan's sweet laughter
Grandad's wisely words
Dad's support
I can't truly leave these behind

My heart thumping like a drum
The boat leaves the harbour
I'll never see this country again
Nor them either.

Ayesha Khan (13)
Westwood Language College For Girls

MY MUM

She is like sunshine on a cloudy day,
She is my shoulder to cry on,
She is as scatty as a cat,
She is my rock that keeps me going,
She is as firm as a newly-built wall,
She is a party animal,
She is as cheeky as a monkey,
She is a world of imagination,
She is like a hurt bird never giving up,
She is a handful of emotions,
She is as loving as a mother can be,
She is an animal in a cage just waiting to get out,
She is as crazy as an angry rhino,
She is a delicate flower,
She is as beautiful as can be,
She is a book that is always open,
She is a bag with everything I need in it,
She is perfect in every way, because she is my mum.

Coral Jamieson (12)
Westwood Language College For Girls

LAST LESSON OF THE DAY

When will the buzzer buzz and stop this boredom?
We're like a pack of unruly wolves,
Because the teacher cannot teach us things that we dislike to learn.
I'm tired of her forcing us to learn.

I love to write rudeness, chat and do messy work that I give
to Miss Fletcher,
I can't see what good it is to me or the teacher.

I will not waste my time on this,
I don't care about doing things badly!
What is the point of Miss Fletcher teaching us?

I know I can describe a description of a lion, but what is the point?
Why does the teacher care so much about us?
Why shouldn't I write rudeness and chat?
I'll talk to my friends until the buzzer goes.

Jemma Haynes (13)
Westwood Language College For Girls

A PAIN IN THE HEART

At first I was angry,
But that anger became pain,

I thought I could try to forget about it,
But it all stayed the same.

I was so blind to think
Friendship could never fall apart,
It didn't for me because it all stayed in my heart.

I arrived after that and checked my phone,
There was nothing there.
Oh, I felt so alone!

But suddenly there was a beep,
It was a message from you.

It was so sweet, cute and warm . . .
I want to be friends too!

Catarina Ribeiro (13)
Westwood Language College For Girls

MY MUM

She is like a diamond, precious and divine,
She is a flower planted in my heart,
She is like an eagle flying freely,
She is a book ready to be read,
She is like a blanket, warm and soft,
She is a carving in my life,
She is like a lioness standing strong and tall,
She is a problem solver for all my needs,
She is like a seed growing to please,
She is a friend to help and never gives up,
She is like a ray of light leading the way,
She is a butterfly, beautiful and lovely,
She is like an arrow, pointing me in the right direction.

Stephanie Donovan (12)
Westwood Language College For Girls

DISAGREE

The government wanted to change the country
We disagreed
They were going to change the way we live
We disagreed
They were going to knock down our house and build something else
We disagreed
That is why I am here all alone, on my own
Don't disagree
Next time I won't.

Shikiera Betts (13)
Westwood Language College For Girls

My Answer Still Remains The Same

If I was to leave behind something
I'd leave behind something trivial
It would have to be my nail polish and phone
As well as my home
But what would I bring
Nothing can ever replace
It would have to be my family
They are kind and loving and thanked by God
For doing no sin and being no sinners
To hear my family call my name
Is a treasure every day
So you can ask me a million times
But my answer still remains the same.

Jadine Rose Baltram (12)
Westwood Language College For Girls

There Is No Choice

Pen and paper I could do without
Not writing for a month I could do
EastEnders I would miss
But the wonderful love between my sisters and I,
I would not lose.

Aliyah is my joy, my world and my pride
Although it does not show, she is my Siamese twin.
Khayira is the same but more loving
I know what I would leave
My pen and paper
But not my family.

Kamiesha Mayne (12)
Westwood Language College For Girls

FORGOTTEN MEMORIES

'Daddy they're coming,
They're coming to get you,'
'Don't worry
They can't split this family apart,'
That's what he said
Before they killed him
Mum was crying
Tissues soaked with tears
They killed him
On the spot
I was standing, I was standing
Feeling sad and alone
We must go
Because now, we are refugees.

Jade Ashman (14)
Westwood Language College For Girls

FIZZY DRINK

Fizz, fizz,
Fizz down your throat,
Sparkling look, sparkling taste,
A liquid that rushes down your throat,
Cools, cools, cools you down like no one can.
You see splashes of sparkling pops bounce out of the cup.
You must enjoy your fizz, fizz,
Like I do myself.

Nathiya Murugaiah (11)
Westwood Language College For Girls

I Am . . .

I am a passion fruit, sweet and caring,
I am a bunch of red grapes, lovely and sharing.

I am a tulip, growing in height,
I am lavender, not always purple by sight.

I am a Lexus, stylish and cool,
I am a Mercedes convertible, on the road I rule.

I am summer, time to dress down,
I am winter you know when I'm around.

I am the Sydney Opera House, I have class,
I am a building made fully out of glass.

I am Barbados, friendly and bright,
I am a remote island with no need to fight.

I am the sun, time to have fun,
I am the rain, you can't see where I've begun.

I am the air, people need me,
I am the earth, water feeds me.

I am Venus, I need people close to me,
I am Pluto, being different is my speciality.

I am a voice, not always loud,
I am a saxophone, my music shows I'm proud.

I am a sandwich, always on the go,
I am chicken, rice and peas, after you eat me I will flow.

I am Dr Pepper, my bottle is curved,
I am wine, best reserved.

I am a tiger, courageous and brave,
I am a polar bear, in my snow cave.

Stephanie Gay (11)
Westwood Language College For Girls

MY NAME MEANS FREE

My name means free
And this is just what I long to be.

I was born in the wilderness,
Nurtured by the breeze,
My only mother was savagery.
Though temperate and kind, neighbours neglected me.
My innocence was robbed and challenged by greed.
Torn from my homelands, I was left to flee.

Like dust in the wind, I dispersed silently.
New lands accepted me but for a fee.
They swallowed my pride and dignity.
They only served me pain and misery.
Now little is left of what was me.
I am one no more, as you can see.

My name means free
And that was just what I longed to be.

Anam-Zahra Mukhtar (13)
Westwood Language College For Girls

I AM . . .

I am a mango; sweet, juicy, in three different colours.
I am a jasmine, smelling succulent and rare.
I am a bus, people are always going to catch me.
I am spring, waking up after a long, cold winter,
When everything I touch starts growing again.
I am Buckingham Palace, standing lofty and fundamental.
I am Madagascar, not very well known, but happy all the same.
I am snow; cold, but can melt a few hearts.

I am water, always making you smile in summer.
I am planet Pluto, not always standing out, but known.
I am a flute, you always know when I'm around
Because of my elegant, exquisite song.
I am a bar of chocolate, most people know and like me.
I am a big bottle of Fanta, very bubbly.
I am a kitten. I love affection, attention and love.

Naomi Driver (11)
Westwood Language College For Girls

LOVE AT FIRST SIGHT

I was outside looking at the sky
all my dreams passed my eyes.
I looked up and saw the twinkle in his eye
I looked down and saw Nike Town upon his feet.
My world passed me so quickly like wind in the sky
I wonder every day why he lies.
One minute he's with me, the next he's with her.
Sometimes I feel like I want to break down and cry
he works this thing I don't know what it is,
it feels like magic upon my heart.
But now I can't let his love go
it hurts, it hurts, like a bullet to my heart
and then as I come home from school I see him with her.
I go to speak to him, he moves aside and I feel like a fool.
I remember the pretty things we used to do together,
we used to cry together, laugh together, share love together.
The way he used to have that pretty smile,
he used to say he cared for me but he was just playing with my mind.
It sends shivers up my spine when I think about the old times.

Timney Batt (14)
Westwood Language College For Girls

My Mum

She is like sunshine, shining her way through the forest leaves.
She is a flower that says her thank yous and pleases.
She is like a boxer fighting her troubles away,
She is a cool breeze on a hot summer's day.
She is like a rabbit leaping above the worst thing,
She is a victim, aware that the worst is happening.
She is like a lioness doing the best for her young,
She is a hard worker, always getting the job done.
She is like a huggable bear,
She is a shining star looking over me everywhere.
She is like a heart bursting with love day by day,
She is a wise owl with amazing things to say.
She is like a thirst-quenching drink in a tall glass,
She is sweet, dark chocolate that will forever last.
She is a bright light from the darkness that isn't mean,
She is my beautiful Nubian queen.

Yasmin Williams (11)
Westwood Language College For Girls

My Life

M y life is not always simple,
Y et I always try to manage.

L aughter is the key that sometimes passes me through.
I   n difficult times it may not do.
F ighting is not the answer so I try my very hardest to ignore,
E ven though I may wish I was dead, I live each day as it comes,
    and more.

Danielle Greene (13)
Westwood Language College For Girls

MEMORIES

She was standing in the playground, all on her own,
Looking so lonely and puzzled,
Sitting on the cold concrete step, alone.

I could tell she had something on her mind.
I wanted to walk over to her,
Another friend she wanted to find.

At lunchtime again, the girl sat
Daydreaming about the times when she had friends.
I wondered why she was wearing that awful hat.

I saw her walking out of the school gates,
Wanting to get as far away as she could, not looking back,
She entered the footpath without any mates.

Then I realised, the memory was of me!

Laura Mitchell (13)
Westwood Language College For Girls

I AM...

I am a mango, bursting with thoughts and ideas,
I am a sunflower, leaning towards the powerful rays of the blazing sun,
I am a plane, soaring swiftly through the cloudy sky,
I am a skyscraper, tall and ambitious,
I am the sea, crashing violently on the rocks, the waves lapping
on the shore,
I am champagne, bubbling rapidly with creative ideas,
I am summer, the rays of sunshine gleaming through the sky,
I am Saturn, a ball of fire with a ring spinning endlessly around it,
Surrounded by millions of sparkling stars,
I am a forest full of wild animals and insects.

Charlotte Scicluna (12)
Westwood Language College For Girls

MY LIFE

This is my life
My so-called life
With boys and girls
And diamonds and pearls.

This is my life
My dangerous life
With gangsters and crews
With don'ts and dos.

This is my life
My boring life
With schools and stuff
And everything tough.

This is my life
My sadness life
With people dying
And everybody crying.

This is my life
My happy life
With laughter and fun
In the bright shining sun.

Zainab Dawodu (13)
Westwood Language College For Girls

MY BEST FRIEND

My best friend is funny,
She also is very bright,
But sometimes she is very scared of heights.

My best friend is very clumsy,
Which makes me smile like the sun,
But our close friendship has just begun.

She can be very sensitive sometimes,
But that is not such a worry
Because every time she needs me,
She knows I will be there in a hurry.

Me and her are like sisters,
We will always stick together,
But I know she will always be
In my heart, forever, ever and ever.

Cayleigh Boome (12)
Westwood Language College For Girls

THERE IS NO CHOICE

There is no choice,
This is the voice of Georgina the refugee speaking,
I'd leave behind,
My green blind, instead of leaving,
The ones who helped when I was teething.
There is no choice,
This is the voice of Georgina the refugee speaking,
I'd leave behind my mint tea, would you agree?
Instead I'd take my pets.
There is no choice,
This is the voice of Georgina the refugee speaking,
I'd leave behind
My dad's fishing hooks,
A couple of interesting books.
You see me and you see them,
So when you slumber in your bed,
Pray in your head
That they can live a peaceful life.

Georgina Parker-Day (12)
Westwood Language College For Girls

A BABY

We waited for you for nine months
And finally you arrived
A beautiful little baby girl, your happy mother cried
With your dark red cheeks, like a warm red rose
Little hands and little feet and even smaller toes
Then your eyes so bright and blue, like the sky so fresh and new
Your hair deep brown, so soft to touch
This baby girl doesn't ask for much
Then you smile and start to grin
This is where your life will begin
I remember your first tooth, then your first step
I remember your first curl and when you wept
Now you're nearly one year old
And the story of your birthday cannot be kept.

Donna Burnett (13)
Westwood Language College For Girls

I AM ...

I am a green apple, tangy and exotic,
I am a red rose, full of love and care.
I am a motorbike, zooming to my target,
I am a summer's day, shining out with all my energy.
I am the Empire State Building, tall and firmly planted,
I am America, been through hell and know what I want.
I am water, I go along and try to put out all the existing flames,
I am planet X, newly discovered and crowded.
I am a lioness fighting for my right to be me.

Iram Qureshi (11)
Westwood Language College For Girls

I AM . . .

I am a strawberry, sweet and delicious
I am a rose, precious and kind
I am a Porsche, zooming, swarming up the steep hill
I am summer, warm and bright
I am the Empire State Building, standing tall over the city below me
I am New York city, loud and getting the message about
I am the snow, cold but full of excitement
However, I am also fire, warm and snugly
I am the galaxy, always finding new planets
I am a trumpet, loud and proud
I am the countryside, quiet when I want to be
I am rice, soft and unique
I an coke, fizzy and bubbly
And I am a dolphin, splashing through life with a cheeky grin
                                        on my face.

   I am me, I wonder what I will be next?

Zahra Budhwani (12)
Westwood Language College For Girls

THE TRIP

A pencil sharpener went on a trip,
He sailed, he flew and occasionally skipped.
Along with a mouse, with flaming red hair,
Look out for them here, look out for them there.
Until one day they spied a brown bear,
Who ate them both up with baked beans for a dare.

Lucyanna Pearse (11)
Westwood Language College For Girls

My Mum

She is like a ray of sunshine, showing me the way.
She is a diary, you can share secret things and she'll never tell.
She is like a tree giving you shelter from the rain.
She is a butterfly, always pretty.
She is like a computer, always hard at work.
She is a friend, someone you can fall back on.
She is like a business woman, because she has a flash car!
She is a flower, always smelling sweet.
She is like a book, always interesting.
She is the sun, never ceases to make anyone smile or laugh.
She is like a deserted island, always a surprise around the corner.
She is a birthday party, which comes with loads of presents
                                            and surprises.

Latifah McFarlane (11)
Westwood Language College For Girls

My Mum

She is like a teddy bear, always there to give you a hug and a kiss.
She is a sunny morning, always there to cheer you up.
She is like a delicate flower, always with a beautiful scent.
She is a walking telephone, always there to sort out your problems
                                            and listen to your stories.
She is like an angel, singing softly when she speaks to you.
She is a wise owl, helping me with my homework.
She is like a rainbow, shining bright after a rainy morning.
She is a giant butterfly, fluttering swiftly on a golden, crisp morning.
She is like a rare jewel, precious and one of a kind.
She is an eagle, always making sure I am all right.
She is like spring, introducing happiness after winter.
She is a queen in my heart.

Sophie Padbury (11)
Westwood Language College For Girls

THE NEW BABY

I remember I was in hospital,
I couldn't remember why,
I heard a baby cry,
And the nurse came running by.

I went in to see my mum,
Her tummy had a great big bump.
I saw a baby, my dad explained
That the baby was ours.

I asked my mum, 'Is it a boy or girl?'
My mum replied, 'She's a girl.'
I now had a baby sister
And my body went down with blisters.

That's the end, but for me
It's a new beginning.

Kayleigh Baker (13)
Westwood Language College For Girls

I KNOW WHAT I WOULD LEAVE

I know what I would leave,
I would leave behind my toothbrush
And I would bring my Bible and my family,
To hear the voices calling mine
And the voices I am used to,
To read the words of God,
For the words to comfort me
And me knowing that I am safe at all times
Because God is with me,
I know what I would leave,
My toothbrush.

Bianca Gordon (12)
Westwood Language College For Girls

How Can I Forget?

September 11th,
How can I forget?
The day when terrorists struck,
The day when many nationalities died,
The day when America lost part of its greatest pride,
The day when people had to face their death,
The day when America held its breath,
The day when people's lives had to end,
The day when we couldn't say goodbye to families and friends.
How can I forget?

Thousands of lives had come to an end,
Families and friends had cried,
Mothers, fathers, brothers, sisters, husbands and wives
Couldn't say goodbye,
The pain their loved ones felt, couldn't describe in words
To know that they are really gone, couldn't be seen or heard.

Day and night firemen worked tirelessly, risking their lives,
Just one more rescue, they thought, as time passed by.
Loved ones prayed, loved ones cried,
Wishing their lost ones would come alive.

Every day and every night they try
To reminisce their happy times.
Days and weeks and months have passed by,
They still don't accept their loved ones are lost.

Sonya Dunkley (13)
Westwood Language College For Girls